FASHION DOLL MAKEOVERS

Learn from the Artists

by Jim Faraone

Published by Hobby House Press, Inc.
Grantsville, Maryland 21536

DEDICATION

To David W. Simpson for his support, encouragement, friendship, and his belief in my creativity. Thanks for guiding me into the field of designing for the public David!

ACKNOWLEDGEMENTS

Besides all the featured artists/designers, I'd like to thank the following people who deserve a heart-felt thank you for their support and help with this book: my father and mother, Albert and Florence Faraone for their support; my nephew Charles Faraone whose computer expertise helped tremendously in the book assembly; Cindy Kent for photographing the creations of Ricky LaChance and Ann Meili; Barbara Miller of *Miller's Price Guide* for her guidance; David Folkman for the photograph of Barb Rausch; Les Bidrawn for photographing the creations of Barb Rausch; David W. Simpson for allowing his collection of Mark Ouellette creations be photographed; Eric Lucas for photographing the creations of Jean Haskett; Jeff Nestor for photographing the creations of James Bogue; Becky Asher for photographing the creations of Steven Taranto; Kerry Anne Faraone for photographing the "How To" series; Barry Sturgill; Judith Whorton for photographing the creations of Anthony Ferrara; David Ramsey for the photograph of Charles L. Mo; and Dan Lippit for photographing the creations of Dorinda Balanecki.

Front Cover: (Top) An innovative team creation by Ken Bartram and Don Meindl. Ken Bartram is the make-up and hair artist, while Don Meindl designs the costume. (Bottom) A Mel Odom Gene™ doll. (Left) A James Bogue Bild-Lili in a black dress.

Title Page: A Bill Waldow creation.

Introduction Page: Italian BARBIE® doll with a total face repaint by Dorinda Balanecki.

Back Cover: A Joshard Originals creation.

Fashion doll models: BARBIE® and Ken® are trademarks of Mattel, Inc.; Gene® is by Mel Odom; Paige™ is by Robert Tonner; Dr. X™ is a trademark of Hasbro; Jenny™ is a trademark of Takara, Japan

ABOUT THE AUTHOR

JIM FARAONE, an avid BARBIE® collector, has a collection of over 3,000 BARBIE® dolls and related items. He is not only a BARBIE® doll collector but also collects modern dolls, paper dolls, paper toys, and miniatures. His diverse collection even includes 1950's plastic doll house furniture and celebrity autographed photos.

Jim publishes his own quarterly publication on paper dolls titled *Paper Doll Pal*, a publication featuring old, new, and future paper dolls and the original artwork of paper doll artists today.

A respected artist, Jim has had his artwork featured twice in the UFDC publication *Doll News*. His artwork has also been the featured souvenir at the North Carolina Paper Doll Convention and been on display at the Metropolitan Museum of Art in New York City several years ago. He also created a paper doll of "Striker", the 1994 World Cup Soccer mascot, which appeared in papers around the world.

His articles on the BARBIE® doll and paper dolls have appeared in *Contemporary Doll Collector*. He has also covered the BARBIE® doll Convention and Paper Doll Convention for this publication.

Jim is internationally known in the collecting field and is actively involved with many of the conventions. He organizes and runs many of the Artist's Galleries which feature the new work of professional and non-professional artists. Jim is an avid believer in supporting the artists and giving them the recognition they deserve. Jim has been commended numerous times for his determination in giving the artists a place in the spotlight. He has also ran numerous workshops on painting techniques, paper doll artwork, and the recreation of the fashion doll, taking each budding artist step-by-step through the trials and tribulations of creating.

Jim and his collectibles have appeared in several magazines and newspapers around the world. His most fun recollection is being featured on the front page of *USA Today* which featured him kissing a life size mannequin of the BARBIE® doll.

His recreated fashion dolls have also appeared on several television news segments and in newspapers. His next goal is to present the artist's work on national television.

Jim Faraone has made his hobbies a lifetime infatuation and the joy, comfort, and friendships he's made over the years are always treasured. He truly enjoys hearing from collectors around the world.

Additional copies available @ $19.95 plus postage from

HOBBY HOUSE PRESS, INC.
www.hobbyhouse.com
1 Corporate Drive
Grantsville, MD 21536
1-800-554-1447
E-mail: hobbyhouse@gcnet.net

©1996 Jim Faraone
2nd Printing — September 1999

688.7
221
Fara

Printed in the United States of America

ISBN: 0-87588-471-7

TABLE OF CONTENTS

ARTIST n. A person who practices the fine arts of painting, sculpture, etc.

FASHION n. The mode or manner of dress, living, and style that prevails in society, especially in high society; good form or style; current style or custom; a piece of clothing made up in the current style, fashionable, fashionableness adj. fashionably adv.

DESIGN v. To draw and sketch preliminary outlines; to invent or create in the mind; to have as an intention or goal. n. An artistic or decorative piece of work; a project; a plan; a well thought-out intention. designedly adv.

DESIGNER n. One that creates and manufactures a new product style or design; esp: one who designs and manufactures high-fashion clothing.

INTRODUCTION

Many of us have had dreams of the ultimate fashion doll — a doll that fulfills all our own dreams and fantasies; a doll which allows our creative imaginations to run wild with excitement. There are many wonderful fashion dolls on the market today, but these are designed and produced with the mass market in mind and not for the individual collector who has desires of his own.

There are also those who wish to restore the beauty of their childhood dolls. Those cherished, love-worn dolls that gave comfort and unconditional love over the years. Some adored treasures have worn makeup, or a few bald spots, and who knows what, but their value is priceless to each individual.

The reasons for makeover or redux dolls are endless. It may be a way to express the bottled up creativity in each one of us. It could be the excitement of seeing our thoughts transformed onto a three-dimensional figure. It could be seeing that doll from childhood transformed into the beauty she once was. It could be a feeling of accomplishment as you step back, take in the splendor of your new creation and say, "Hey, I did that!"

You can find dolls to makeover at flea markets, doll shows, attics, basements, toy shops, or wherever your heart may lead you on the hunt. Many makeover artists prefer to purchase new fashion dolls so they can show their support to the companies and individuals who have created beautiful fashion dolls over the years. That's because most of them are collectors, and they invest their earnings in more fashion dolls to preserve their own private collections.

This book will take you on a journey to creating your own dream doll fantasies. Fashion wise, it's up to you and your imagination. Will you take the road of Haute Couture and fabulous evening wear, or take a side road to the world of Fantasy? Many may take the route of the eras and create ensembles of the '50s, '60s, and so on. There are others who may fancy ethnic costumes to display their heritage. No matter what you decide to design, the satisfaction you'll receive will astound you. No one becomes a master designer overnight. Many of the artists/designers featured will confirm that it's a matter of trial and error to achieve your final goal. We've all been there and are still experimenting, but it's an experience that has given us much pleasure and satisfaction.

To inspire your creative juices, I have showcased 34 talented individuals whose extraordinary talents have raptured collectors throughout the years. The craftsmanship and minute details of their creations have astounded even the most avid doll collector.

Their creative ideas have been used by leading manufacturers which is an unconventional honor to say the least.

Fashion Doll Makeovers will bring these artists/designers and their creations into the well deserved spotlight. Each taking a solo bow as they present their artistic background, creations, and passion for designing.

This book is just a representation of their fashion creations. These talented individuals are constantly coming up with new ideas and techniques. Their ability to create is endless.

The artists/designers featured are not affiliated in any way with the companies that produce the dolls that their fashions are displayed on. These dolls are merely "used" as mannequins.

If you are interested in finding out more about each individual artist, please send them a SASE with one extra loose stamp. The artists would be delighted to hear your response to their work.

Let's step into the miniature world of Haute Couture, Fantasy, Ethnic, Vogue and those creations that can only let the imagination soar beyond ecstasy!

Read on...

Dolls are magical caricatures of people. With their beauty, grace, and expressive faces, dolls remind us of a never-never land of nostalgic childhood memories, a place many of us had to leave behind as we grew up. To many collectors, dolls represent a return to that world of innocence.

This book showcases artists' interpretations of beauty and love for dolls. As you look at the hundreds of different examples and consider how you wish to design your own doll — face, hair, costume, accessories — the author and publisher would like you to do the following :

• CAUTION — Any change to the originality of a doll can influence its resale value to a collector on the secondary market, we therefore suggest you use much loved and much played with dolls in your artistic endeavor. Using these "hurt" dolls is rescuing and preserving them for future generations. If you can not find much loved or played with dolls then use newly made dolls.

• Always sign and date your work. This makes your design an original and ensures that all your hard work and dedication will be recognized.

• Represent the sale of your work as coming from you the artist — never represent yourself as "Jim's Barbie® doll and outfits","Ginger's Gene® dolls", etc. Although you have created your own design for a fashion doll, that fashion doll was originally created by and the rights to the doll belong to someone else. Include a disclaimer, such as the following, in your advertising and show displays: <u>Doll name</u> is a trademark of <u>Company name</u>. This (These) doll(s) are not sponsored by or affiliated with <u>Company name</u>.

• Most importantly, enjoy yourself and let your creative juices flow!

BARB RAUSCH

I have been a *KATY KEENE COMICS* fan since 1954, and received the "Katy Keene Designer of the Year" award from Bill Woggon in 1959. I earned a B.A. in Art Education and an M.A. from Michigan State University in 1963 and 1968, and taught grade school art in Flint, Michigan public schools for 17 years.

The founder of Katy Keene Fandom in 1980, I began working as a professional comics and commercial artist in 1982. Along with credits in many different comics and related publications, I have worked on two seasons of JEM show storyboards and drawn BARBIE® doll coloring books and paper dolls, as well as other paper dolls for Golden/Western. Since 1991 I have been a regular artist drawing BARBIE™ comics for Marvel/Mattel, and nine covers for *BEAUTY AND THE BEAST* comics for Marvel/Disney.

My collecting has focused on contemporary BARBIE® dolls, with one exception: rooted-hair Ken® dolls. In

Disney's John Smith as Sala'i, an actual historical personage, the ward of Leonardo da Vinci. *Photo by David Folkman.*

pursuit of these Ken® dolls, I discovered the 1980 Sport and Shave Ken® dolls that came with a variety of hair textures - many of which didn't survive children's play. To deal with the damaged hair, I decided to totally remove the hair and put on one of my own 3/4 inch-size wigs.

With my mannequin properly wigged, I delved into 17th century male costume and reinterpreted it on the doll as accurately as possible.

Finding tiny buttons, buckles, accessories, and trims, gets easier all the time as doll show exhibitors cater to the creator's market, but I prefer to make my own patterns and to exercise as much ingenuity as possible with my tiny accessories. For example, I construct my leather doublets and Cavalier boots from old leather gloves found at thrift shops, and for flouncy shirts, I use vintage handkerchiefs.

To get back to my creative "roots", I plan to redesign the BARBIE® doll as Katy Keene using Mattel's Western Stompin' Tara Lynn doll.

Barb Rausch
9402 Glen Oaks Circle
Sun City, AZ 85351-1401

Photos by Les Bidrawn.

Creations by **BARB RAUSCH**

Dion Constantine is a fantasy personality of a Venetian aristocrat of the 17th century.

Photos by Les Bidrawn.

Even as the youngest in a family of five in the '60s, I still grew up being on my own, spending much of my time on designing outfits for Katy Keene (my favorite), Millie the Model, and sometimes even Betty and Veronica of the Archies. The BARBIE® doll was not easily found in the Philippines then, so I was content with comics and paper doll books. One of my favorites was a little Golden book of Sleeping Beauty which came with a set of paper dolls right out of the Disney movie (I'm still searching for its replacement today!). I remember asking my mom to please get me an 18 inch titian fashion doll with breasts in a pair of panties and red pumps, but instead was given a white handled cowboy gun.

I finally met my first BARBIE® doll, which was a brunette bend leg Francie™ doll, in 1966 (and yes, even then her arms were already pale white). She came with the Skipper® doll's *Hearts and Flowers* outfit. I was thrilled with the granny glasses, the yellow realistic looking purse, (and yes they were a bit tight and short on her, but who cares!) micro mini skirts. I was really happy because this doll with her eyelashes and her ladylike sitting position with bended knees and slight crossing of the legs (no more spread eagle sitting position like the cheap imitation ones) looked real. Next came *Golden Glory* which was a disappointment for the Francie™ doll as I had to stuff her up with tissue. Then came a Live Action P.J.® doll, and of course I was hooked. What impressed me the most was the details and attention given to the doll's outfits.

My mom was a seamstress in her teens during World War II in the Philippines. Growing up I watched her sew all these neat outfits with her foot pedaled Singer. I tried it when she was away and I could not even move the fabric by more than an inch, it just went back and forth and so on. I just could not operate the machine by foot. So on one of my mother's birthdays, I gave her a motor to attach to the machine and my sewing career began.

While most boys were studying carpentry, auto mechanics, etc. during Summer School, I enrolled myself in a tailoring class. With the rest of the class content with just making a white sleeve shirt, I was blessed to have an instructor who encouraged me to design a shirt that had cuts, tucks, pleats, and an epaulette here and there, which helped me gain a better understanding of the construction of garments.

I started making the BARBIE® doll acceptable to my family by dressing them as Christmas angels and a nativity scene, in that, it did not look like I was playing with them, but was making them as decorative art. I would also photograph them with my twin lens Yashica mat camera because I told my family I wanted to be a fashion photographer when I grew up. Little did they know.

Here I am in my forties. I have always been asked if any of my originals like the Scarlett set I did back in 1989, before Mattel caught onto the idea, would be for sale. At the time, I never had the time to do another one and also knew that I would be bored if all I was doing was reproduction. With enough requests and encouragement, I decided to do it, and that's how Couture came about.

"Marilyn"

Franklin Lim Liao
1035-C South Van Ness
San Francisco, CA. 94110

Creations by
FRANKLIN LIM LIAO

Each design is usually inspired by a combination of the fabric and a style that I saw in a magazine or an inspiration. Just like painting, I start with a basic pattern and while executing the design I envision the technical aspect required to get that flair or that fold to achieve the form. Then I hand sew the individual trims, fur, buttons, and snaps (sorry I don't believe in Velcro, that's the easy way out). Shoes are created using the same material and then the finishing accessories such as a hat, purse, jewelry, and gloves are added. Hair is curled and styled to match and makeup is applied. Each doll is packed with my signature black stand ready for display with the new proud owner. On the average, each doll takes about eight to sixteen hours to finish, and then I take on another new design.

Now even in my sleep, I will be dreaming about what my next creation will be like and in turn, realizing a childhood dream.

"Madonna"

8

RICKY LACHANCE

Do you have a lot of BARBIE® nostalgic goddess' and wish to dress them in couture-ly gowns or suits? Just call LaRicky Originals and Coutures. My gown/suit creations are like those of Chanel, Dior, Balaenciaga, Lacroix, Versace, and I. Mizrahi in design.

Born on August 18, 1963, I grew up with television. I loved watching "The Carol Burnett Show" and "The Sonny and Cher Show". Their costumes amazed my eyes, yet I never knew who created them. Because of an illness, I was totally deaf. I never heard Carol and Cher's singing, but their costumes interested me as their shiny, beaded, and sequined gowns moved gracefully.

Years later I started collecting the BARBIE® doll. I kept my first Irish International on my nightstand for many years. Since 1986, I have purchased many BARBIE® and friends. I really was a closet BARBIE® doll collector as my family didn't find out until my collection grew big. I'll never forget my mother's reaction when I told her, but today she and the rest of my family support my hobby. I have cut down my spending, purchasing only the limited edition dolls in designer coutures, the Happy Holiday and Christmas theme doll. I do look forward to the Hallmark special editions for other holidays like Valentine's day, Easter, etc.

My most favorite doll is the Bob Mackie BARBIE® doll and now I know who created those costumes for Carol and Cher!

How did I decide to become a designer/artist? I went to the fabric store to buy needles for my mother. I curiously looked around at every shelf stocked with fabrics. I loved to touch every thread of every fabric, but I was too chicken to sew a dress. As a subscriber to a BARBIE® doll magazine (I'm also an avid reader of Billyboy's *BARBIE®, Her Life and Times* which is worn from my frequent readings!) I fell in love with the handmade outfits designers created for the BARBIE® doll. I looked for ads which advertised handmade outfits by collectors. I wrote to each one and requested couture or one-of-a-kind gowns. Unfortunately all the replies were copied outfits from the BARBIE® doll's 900 and 1600 fashion series, plus plantation gowns from the movie *Gone With The Wind*.

My friends and customers ask me about how I envision such wonderful designs. I always choose the fabrics first and let my imagination run wild rather than start with a sketch. Solid and mini prints are the best bet. I never choose out-of-style fabrics or ones with big patterns. I always watch every fashion television program like "Style"

with Elsa K., FTV, "Videofashion", etc. For many years, every week I got ideas from these shows and then created my own designs.

I favor the nostalgic BARBIE® doll over the newer dolls. Why? Because I find it simpler to dress the nostalgic dolls with 1900 to 1950 style outfits. By mixing and matching different patterns, I can create my own design. I even add finishing touches, i.e. jewelry, gloves, purses and hats.

One of my favorite designers and the first designer I have met is Bob Mackie. I fell in love with his first BARBIE® doll (Mackie Gold) and the next year (1991) I presented him with my first designed doll "Holiday Glamour" in Center City, Philadelphia, PA. The next month I received a surprise package from Bob Mackie himself. It was a rejected sketch Bob drew for Mattel, Inc. who produced his series. It will hang in my room forever and I will always be his pen pal.

In December of 1995, in Hasbrouck Height, NJ., Bob Mackie made a presentation at a BARBIE® doll sale. I didn't know if Bob would notice me again. He did, and he was so happy that he hugged me in front of all the collectors. Some were surprised and some had

A nostalgic BARBIE® doll models a Dior-styled gown with pearls.

LaRicky Originals and Coutures
Ricky LaChance
111 West Germantown Ave.
Maple Shade, NJ. 08052

Photos by Cindy Kent.

Creations by
RICKY LaCHANCE

Kinky BARBIE® doll in Betsy Johnson's gown.

blank expressions on their face. I waited in line to get his rare signature and when it was my turn, I presented him with my new designed doll "LaRicky Christmas Beauty". He loved her so much that he told me that when he got home, he would put my doll on the shelf with the other dolls I gave him. I was thrilled about that.

When I'm not creating LaRicky Originals and Coutures, I am an avid collector of Christmas tree pins. I have over 100+ pins from vintage to brand new. My friends and customers send them as Christmas gifts. Once I receive a pin, I wear it and then I put it in one of my display boxes to treasure it. Rhinestone pins are my favorite, but if I see a wacky or "out-of-art" one, I must buy it, but not all. I always collect Bob Mackie's pins from "Wearable Art by Bob Mackie" on QVC. I also have a few items like ties, scarves, and vests by him.

Wicked eyed BARBIE® doll wears Pam Dennis' 1995 Oscar gown.

My favorite color is fuchsia. Fuchsia is rich, sexy, and seductive. Purple, black, and blue were my original colors until the Franklin Mint released the 18 inch fashion doll in a stunning gown of fuchsia and black by you know who.

LaRicky Originals and Coutures will present new lines for the 11-1/2 inch goddess and the 12 inch hunk. My outfits sell at the "In The Spotlight" store in San Francisco, CA as well as in other stores in other states. Experience the magic of LaRicky Originals and Coutures.

LaRicky models wear his color —Fuchsia

Halloween Belle won second prize by DVBC.

Photos by Cindy Kent.

MARK P. MIDDENDORF

I've been collecting BARBIE® dolls since 1981. My collection is constantly shifting but I always have 250-300 dolls as my permanent part. My favorite head mold is the Steffie/Whitney doll head, with the Black Steffie being my favorite of all.

I received my B.F.A., Fashion Design at Parsons School of Design in 1987. I have been sewing for BARBIE® dolls since 1989 but only began to sell my work in 1994. It wasn't until 1995 that I started to really concentrate on those all important essentials — **accessories**. Now my creations have gloves, jewelry, handbags, pantyhose, etc.

I am becoming known for my rooted, long hair Ken® dolls in fantasy, winged costumes. I have been doing reroots for about five years now. I can credit all my painting and rooting skills to MiKelman, who has been gracious enough to share his skills with me.

Paul David and MiKelman have been my good friends the last few years and because of their encouragement I finally started doing shows and selling my work. I plan to sell clothing separately and concentrate on truly spectacular, beaded ensembles with masks. My one-of-a-kind rerooted and costumed dolls will be limited so I can concentrate on some of my other sewing projects.

**Mark P. Middendorf
2600 S.W. Williston Rd., #1523
Gainesville, FL 32608**

Creations by
MARK P. MIDDENDORF

KEN BARTRAM

My parents were not the type to want me to have dolls. However, I had other plans in mind. I just waited until I became an adult and got all the dolls I could afford. As a child, I really just wanted one - the "Solo In The Spotlight" BARBIE® doll. A female friend at school had the doll and I wanted one. My mother thought it was too sexy and my father was flipped that I wanted a DOLL! So, I forgot about the episode and went to female friends homes and played with their BARBIE® dolls. Much later, I went to college (forgetting about my desire to own a BARBIE® doll) and graduated with a B.F.A. in Art Education, which I never used. There were no jobs in teaching art in Memphis, Tennessee so I went to cosmetology school. I enjoyed doing hair but really loved doing makeup. I've been fortunate to have made-up wonderful celebrities, many brides, and beautiful models. I'm glad things worked out the way they did.

When I finished school, I began collecting odd but beautiful things to put on some large shelves I had built. I loved things for their color and texture. Then, a friend gave me an old bubblecut in the gold and white brocade outfit. I put it on the shelf wondering if BARBIE® dolls were still made. We went to a toy store and saw aisles of BARBIE® dolls. This was in 1976 and I bought a Superstar BARBIE® just to have a new BARBIE® doll to go with the old BARBIE® doll. I bought a few more, then a few more, and a few more. All of you know the rest. I had tons of BARBIE® dolls. After so many smiling blond faces, I began to like the BARBIE® doll's friends

better than the BARBIE® doll. My favorite is still the Steffie-P.J.-Whitney doll head mold. This doll has been created as White, Black, Hispanic, and Asian with a multitude of hair colors. That is, until the Asian head mold came out. I enjoy the Asian as much as the Steffie-P.J.-Whitney dolls.

I always wanted the dolls to have more color, different hair colors, and rooted eyelashes. I didn't know how to achieve what I wanted. Then, at a doll show in Bradenton, Florida, I met Michael Alexander and Paul David from Ohio. Paul and I had met over the telephone. I really enjoy talking to Paul to this day. He's funny and a great guy. He showed me a mermaid that Michael had made for him with long corkscrew curls and colorful facial paint. It wasn't for sale, I'm sorry to say because I collect all kinds of mermaids plus mermaid dolls. I have a bathroom with mermaids all over it. I have mermaid everything, like posters, paper dolls, magnets, and etc. Anyway you get the mermaid fetish picture. Michael had faith in me that I could do a rerooting with patience and practice. This is how I began — rerooting, then repainting. I was awful at first, but I learned how to get the results I wanted with practice (and 4X magnification). Now all the dolls I own are repainted, eyelashed, and rerooted. I just can't help myself! I owe a lot to Michael - he gave me the practical knowledge of "how to do". Many thanks to MiKelman!

I also have the Mel Odom Gene® dolls. They are a 15 inch fash-

Ken Bartram
6203-D Markstown Drive
Tampa, FL 33617

ion doll that look like a '40s movie star. I have always been a fan of Mel Odom's artwork and I love these dolls! They have the glamour and quality and size that I really like. My "Gene" dolls have also been repainted and lashes applied, hair cut and styled. I like the shorter hair (like the Gene®'s have) on fashion dolls - I'm always cutting and restyling the doll's hair to get a more fashionable look. I like my mermaids to all have long hair but not my fashion ones!

The clothes for "Gene" are wonderful and styled like the '40s, and you can buy extra outfits! Very elegant. Just like the clothes I would make if I could sew. Unfortunately, I cannot sew! I must depend on others, like Don Meindl, for that talent. Don and I began putting our efforts together creating dolls. He created clothes for the dolls I made up. So, my dolls often have Don's clothing on them, which makes them very well dressed!

I also own the 20 inch Robert Tonner dolls. These are very elegant and dressed beautifully. I've met Robert in Anna Maria, Florida at "Anything Goes" and what a great guy! He is a very talented sculptor and clothes designer. And yes, I've even repainted and rewigged his dolls. He was very gracious about his designs being redone and even signed them for me. I find a serene look on the face of Robert's dolls, which is what I like about the "Gene" dolls and the Mattel Asian dolls. Robert's dolls also have a very realistic sense in their sculpture. Keep up the great work, Robert!

I live happily in Tampa, Florida with my partner, David: his dachshund, Scooter and my Siamese cat, Micio and of course - many dolls!

Asian head mold.

Mel Odom's Gene® doll.

Paige™ by Robert Tonner.

Outfits by Don Meindl.

DON MEINDL

I have always been interested in fashion. As a child, I enjoyed comic book and newspaper character dolls. I attempted to reproduce them using the various fashion dolls of the period. With bits of ribbon, lace, socks, and whatever else I could find, I wrapped my dolls and made dresses and fashion outfits. Gradually I learned to sew and began making real clothes for the dolls.

My inspiration later came as I read Oleg Cassini's weekly articles in the newspaper. He always described the latest trends. I would then make a doll dress, reproducing the fashion of the week.

Upon graduating from High School, I attended Columbus College of Art and Design and Ohio State School of Cosmetology.

Today as a beauty salon owner, I continue to keep my interest in fashion doll clothing. I have presented displays of dolls in Historical, Nostalgic, Ethnic, Military, and Fantasy costumes which I have made. These presentations which include my handmade outfits, stories, poems, doll biographies, historical and technical information, have appeared in various libraries, schools, hospitals, churches, doll shows, television programs, and newspapers. I also enjoy re-creating special event dolls for weddings, anniversaries, and holidays for friends and patrons. With the help of makeup artist Ken Bartram these special dolls are made to look just like the real people they are intended to represent, as he repaints features and restyles their hair.

I am pleased that my doll fashions are enjoyed by patrons from as far away as California to Canada and Puerto Rico to Germany. I enjoy hand making all of the appropriate tiny accessories such as gloves, handbags, jewelry, hats and matching hosiery. These outfits, without the doll, are very reasonably priced.

Don Meindl
7031 Cedarhurst Dr. #3
Fort Myers, FL 33919

A portrait of a real couples's wedding

Creations by
DON MEINDL

MARK OUELLETTE

At the age of 11, Mark designed his first BARBIE® outfit. His cousin, Diane was spending the summer with his family and had brought along a BARBIE® doll to keep his G.I. Joe® doll company. As they played together they switched their dolls back and forth, and it was on one of these occasions when his budding design talents came out in the form of an outfit created with a piece of tinfoil encasing the doll from armpits to ankles. He thought it was the most glamorous thing he'd ever seen. "Actually, she resembled a skinny potato ready for baking", Mark joked.

But his interest in design and couture was piqued and later, after years of fashion design study, he returned to that original 11-1/2 inch model as a "client".

Mark, who did free-lance work for Mattel, loved creating for the BARBIE® doll. "For one," he said, "She always has a consistent figure, she never gains weight. In fact, she never complains and she can be sewn into outfits without the fuss of zippers. More importantly though, she has the unique ability to 'be' the right personality for each outfit I design for her. She can be demure, kittenish, or a vamp, but always with a lady-like attitude."

Mark's preference was dressing the BARBIE® doll in '40s and '50s fashions with exaggerated couture silhouette. Slimskirted suits, slinky gowns, and full Dior-like formals, cocktail dresses with fabulous hats and hostess-wear were his favorites. These were usually executed in fine brocades, silks, and satins.

Mark with his mom Emma.

Mark also enjoyed re-creating costumes from Hollywood's Golden Era. It was always a special challenge for him to match fabrics and prints to an Edith Head or Adrian design from fifty years ago. As with all of Mark's creations, each doll is restyled with the appropriate hairdo and makeup and packaged in a hand-illustrated box.

Mark is no longer with us, but the legacy of his personality and talents will remain with us forever.

You're always in our hearts Mark!

Dolls from the collection of David Simpson.

Creations by
MARK OUELLETTE

Dolls from the collection of David Simpson.

VAL P. DEAN

I am a 43 years old native of Brazil. I have been in the USA since 1976 when I got married. I grew up in Brazil in a middle class family, which included my parents, a brother and a sister. I graduated from college in 1974 with a degree in Communications and worked in public relations for a year. I always loved to travel and decided to explore some new frontiers, which brought me to Denver. I met this wonderful guy, got married, and here I am!

I went back to college and got a second degree in Travel Administration and worked in the travel business until my daughter was born in 1983, a son followed in 1985. I stayed home with the kids until 1992 when I went back to work in the travel business. In 1994 I quit my career in the travel business to pursue my greatest passion — **Collecting BARBIE® Dolls** — full time!

I bought my first BARBIE® doll in 1984, it was a Sun Gold Malibu P.J.® doll. I always loved dolls as a child, especially the adult, full-figure fashion dolls. In Brazil it was very rare to find that type of doll. My sister and I used to transform girl dolls into full-figure dolls with play dough, and also restyle their hair to look like Marilyn Monroe. The last doll I remember having in Brazil was a Suzie Doll, which was a 12 inch fashion doll similar to a Tammy™ doll. I remember being 15 years old and making handmade clothes for this doll.

In addition to my BARBIE® dolls, my collection also contains over 70 BARBIE® doll patterns. I just love to see how the fashions have changed over the years. I also collect paper dolls, mostly fashion and movie star paper dolls. I have some comic magazine paper dolls from when I was a child in Brazil.

I decided to design unique one-of-a-kind Brazilian carnival costumes for the BARBIE® dolls in the summer of 1994. The whole thing took off when I went to the Denver Rocky Mountain Doll Fantasy Show in October that year.

Among all the dealers, I saw the most beautiful, striking table with incredible sophisticated BARBIE® dolls designed by Bill Waldow. I could not believe my eyes! I had only seen dolls like that in BARBIE® magazines, and Bill Waldow's dolls were even prettier. They were perfect! It was like a dream come true. His work encouraged me to pursue my fantasy, to do something exciting with my passion for the BARBIE® dolls. After the show, I sent one of my pictures to Bill, and he wrote back with very supportive and inspiring words. We have been friends since. Meeting Bill and getting to know him has been extremely significant in the pursuit of my BARBIE® doll dream.

I quit my career in the travel business and jumped full-time into

Val P. Dean
Rio de Val Fashions
3831 S. Argonne St.
Aurora, CO. 80013

the doll business. I decided to design carnival costumes based on the Rio de Janeiro famed annual festival. During the four days and nights before Ash Wednesday, Rio throws the world's wildest party with street festivals, parades and people dancing in costumes of incredible creativity and beauty. It is very similar to the Mardi Gras celebration in New Orleans. I had participated in many carnival festivities in Brazil and knew that there was no limit to your imagination and creativity in the design of the costumes. I also had a large collection of Brazilian magazines covering the carnival celebrations for the past years with many ideas, and that was the birth of "Rio de Val Fashions"!

My designs are inspired in the authentic spirit of the Brazilian Carnival. Traditionally a revealing swimsuit is worn, complemented by sequins, beads, feathers, flowers, a fabulous cape, and elaborate head wear. Every creation is a one-of-a-kind design and once a design is sold, it is not duplicated. I start by drawing my idea on paper and then look for the right fabric and trims to match the design and the doll I have in mind. Usually I design my own patterns, but sometimes I don't use a pattern at all. The final product is somehow always different from my original idea because I have so much fun improvising and adding new things as I go. I have so many ideas that usually I am working on two or three designs at a time. It takes two to three days to complete a doll the way I want, because they have to talk to me, I have to feel that they are done. Sometimes one little detail is missing and until I get that perfect, the doll is not finished. I like to create one-of-a-kind doll costumes because most of the time the design is created as I go based on the initial idea. There are many exciting things to try, to add, to experiment, that there is no need to duplicate. I am a very creative person!

I did my first show in June of 1996 and the public reaction was wonderful. Most people that stopped at my table had their mouths opened in awe, words such as, "Wow! Look at these dolls, they are beautiful!" were common throughout the day. It felt incredibly good and validated all my ideas. I also entered a design in the competition and got first place with the judges commenting, "What a fun doll." My second show had a similar wonderful reaction from the public, with one lady buying four dolls on the spot.

I think what makes my designs unique is that as a native Brazilian I have seen and experienced first hand one of the greatest events, the Brazilian Carnival, and I am able to incorporate this tremendous energy and passion that we Brazilians have for this event into the world of the BARBIE® doll. My designs give the BARBIE® doll an international flair, an aura of fantasy, of exotic dreams, of glamour, and glitter. There is no limit to what I can do, because those are costumes meant to satisfy someone's imagination, to transport you to a world of fantasy, fun, romance, mystery, something that only BARBIE® dolls can do.

Designing, collecting, and playing with BARBIE® dolls are wonderful activities for adults. I think we all have dreams and fantasies unrealized and through the BARBIE® dolls we can make them come true. Above all, BARBIE® dolls are beautiful dolls, that can be a tremendous source of enjoyment!

Michael McDonnell/House Of Donn-L

I am often asked how I became involved with designing costumes and fashions that fit the BARBIE® and Ken® dolls. From my earliest memories, I have always had a fascination with miniatures of all kinds. I have tried to analyze what the attraction is and have come to the conclusion that it has to do with control. In our hectic lives we have very little control. Outside forces are always effecting us — from managers and supervisors at our jobs, to natural disasters like earthquakes and fires. As children we have even less control of our environment. We are told when to get and when to go to bed. We have no control of where or when or how. We are hauled around as extensions of our parents. I think that miniatures have been, for me, a way to have some control in my life. No matter what happened outside, I could create a perfect world, where everything would remain the way I created it and not change until I wanted it to change.

This need first manifested itself in building. As a child I loved to build buildings, out of blocks, bricks or clay, it didn't matter. My mom and dad were very supportive of this. They bought every kind of building material you can think of: Lincoln Logs, a Girder and Panel Building Set, Lego blocks, and an erector set. One day while shopping for school clothes, they saw the Mattel Modern Furniture. They were beautifully made pieces, and would be perfect for furnishing my buildings. I remember playing with that furniture for hours on end. It was fun going to the toy store and looking for accessories that I could use with my room settings. My mom went to Mexico and brought back items she found down there. The scale of this furniture happened to be "BARBIE® doll scale".

From an early age my mother noticed my artistic ability. She did all she could to encourage this talent. She made sure I had paint and paper. I remember that she was always so supportive of my artistic endeavor. I took art classes at school as well as studying at the Pasadena Art Museum.

My first recollection with the BARBIE® doll was actually with the Ken® doll. I remember seeing the Ken® doll outfits at the store. I would go to Henry's toy store in Pasadena, and sneak over to the "girls section" where the dolls were. I would try to catch a quick glimpse of the Ken® doll outfits before a sales clerk would come over and ask me if I needed any help. I knew that I couldn't have any of these outfits. Boys did not play with dolls, but I still looked longingly at the little miniatures included with the clothing, thinking of how much fun it would be to have the Ken® doll use them. He could take a "bath", use his razor, soap, and wash cloth. One day my father came home and decided that his son shouldn't be playing with a doll house. I resigned myself, and my miniatures were packed away. In my teens I rediscovered this furniture and started collecting again. After I got my first job, I thought it would be neat to have some "people" to populate my miniature rooms.

I went to Newberry's and

"Sierra High"

Mike McDonnell
309 Concord Street
Unit P
Glendale, CA 91203

Creations by
MICHAEL MCDONNELL

"Latin Holiday"

bought a blond Stacey doll and a couple of outfits. I tried to sneak the doll into the house, but I guess I was not a very good smuggler, because as soon as I got to my room, my mom asked what I had in the bag. To my surprise, she was quite relieved that I had bought a doll and not a knife or booze or something. Not long after that I came down with a chronic case of "BARBIE® Doll Fever". I began to buy BARBIE®, Francie™, and Ken® doll fashions as fast as my pay checks were cashed. I remember hours of guiltless opening of these outfits, and trying them on the dolls.

I continue to collect, new outfits, as well as going to swap meets, and the Salvation Army. I used to go to a special Salvation Army doll store in Long Beach. They collected all the donated dolls and sold them through this outlet. The store had old BARBIE® and Ken® dolls stacked to the ceiling, along with accessories, and outfits. By the mid '80s I had amassed a large collection. I had a special fondness for Ken® and his fashions. I strived to collect every Ken® outfit made from 1961 through 1971. The few items that I still desired, had become prohibitively expensive. It was at this point that I decided that my collecting had to go in a different direction.

I had always admired the early BARBIE® and Ken® dolls outfits, so with my limited sewing knowledge, I tried to sew one. Well needless to say, it didn't turn out very well, but the experience sparked my

"Paris Tour"

"Buttons and Bows"

interest in learning to make my own outfits for the dolls. It soon became evident to me that I needed additional knowledge to create professional looking fashions. I started taking classes in fashion design, sewing, and pattern making. I remember the first outfit that I sold. A collector, who previously purchased only vintage Mattel items, purchased a doll in one of my outfits. I asked why he would buy such a common doll. He told me he was buying it for the outfit, not the doll. I was quite surprised, since to my knowledge serious BARBIE® doll collectors only wanted Mattel made outfits. I began to think maybe I could make outfits and sell them. This would give me money to buy more fabric and supplies.

Thus, The House of Donn-L was born. Since that time I have strived to create fashions that match or exceed the standards set by Mattel's vintage fashions. I envisioned a fashion house for the BARBIE® doll. The name House of Donn-L, is a contraction of my last name McDonnell. New outfit ideas are always challenging. I spend hours, just thinking of how to make a certain outfit or accessory. I love going on buying trips looking for new fabric and supplies that can be made into new creations.

I enjoy creating these miniature fashions, both for the engineering challenge as well as the artistic one. It is not unusual for me to drape a muslin sloper many times before the garment hangs properly. The garments must fit the doll and at the same time be removable. The fashions are real "working" clothing, not permanently affixed on the doll. I produce all of my designs as either, one-of-a-kind or limited editions of no more than thirty pieces. In addition, I have created unique packaging to show off my fashions. There is no end to creative challenges - from outfit conception to display and promotion.

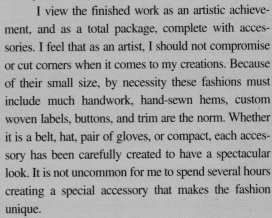

I view the finished work as an artistic achievement, and as a total package, complete with accessories. I feel that as an artist, I should not compromise or cut corners when it comes to my creations. Because of their small size, by necessity these fashions must include much handwork, hand-sewn hems, custom woven labels, buttons, and trim are the norm. Whether it is a belt, hat, pair of gloves, or compact, each accessory has been carefully created to have a spectacular look. It is not uncommon for me to spend several hours creating a special accessory that makes the fashion unique.

My first selling successes, were my tailored suits for the BARBIE® doll, and this remains a large part of my line. In addition to this however, I started to create limited editions for my favorite, the Ken® doll. I feel that the Ken® doll doesn't get nearly enough attention. I have created several limited edition outfits for him including a Fishing outfit and a Golfing outfit. I am planning additional ones for him in the future.

Since I design, manufacture, and package all my fashions myself, the quantity of my output is by most comparisons quite small, The House of Donn-L is truly a labor of love on my part.

JIM FARAONE

Born and raised in the Bronx, New York, I began designing outfits at a young age.

Across the street from the apartment building my family lived in was a dress factory. Every so often I would find a plastic bag of scraps outside the factory's door. One man's garbage is another man's find! I would run home with my new found treasure, confiscate a neighbor's dolls, and dress them. I knew nothing about sewing at the time, so all my creations were pinned together onto the dolls. I thought I was hot stuff!

By the age of 14, I was

designing wedding gowns for family and people in the neighborhood. Every bride that wore one of my creations ended up in divorce. A product of the Bronx or a product of my creativity? So much for that career!

By the age of 18, my artwork was on exhibit at the Metropolitan Museum of Art in New York City. I never went to see the exhibit and to this day I still haven't picked up my artwork!

At 21, I was performing on stage as an actor/singer and dancer. I was also performing at nightclubs. Though I always received great reviews, my funniest memories are the times I fell off the stage, broke my toes, and the other happenings of live theater!

By 22 I was designing costumes and sets for Off-Broadway productions, plus various local stage productions in Westchester, N.Y. I loved terrorizing the prima donnas by making their costumes an inch too small or ridiculing them over the airways during interviews!

When I hit the ripe old age of 23, I was designing jewelry for Anne Klein. I can still draw that darn lion today with my eyes closed.

By 24, I'd appeared on stage, television, radio, and been written about in books, newspapers and magazines. To be featured in a movie would be my next goal.

Though I've accomplished a lot in my life time, there's one thing I haven't done, and that is to get a big ego! I just go through life and try to have fun and experience as much as I can. We're only here once, so make the most of it!

In 1987 I began designing outfits for the BARBIE® doll. These were created specifically for special events and as fund raisers for various charities.

Jim Faraone
19109 Silcott Springs Rd.
Purcellville, VA. 20132

Everyone was impressed with the hand beaded and sequined gowns I created. Each bead and sequin being painstakingly sewn on one at a time.

With encouragement of a friend, David Simpson, in 1994 I began creating and selling my designs to the public.

Each doll takes about two full days to complete. There are a lot of steps to go through to finish one doll. Not many collectors realize all the work that is involved with each creation.

Each one of my designs are one-of-a-kind creations, because I'd get bored creating the same thing over and over again. I make the outfit and then hand bead and sequin it continuously jabbing myself with the needle. At times I have an idea in mind but I do create as I go. Once the doll is done, the accessories are added and she's placed in a box with a special designed logo I created.

A graduate of The School of Visual Arts in New York City, I majored in fashion illustration. It was a fun experience, but I'm a firm believer that you truly learn from experiencing things in life and not just attending a prestigious school and coming out with a fancy paper.

Over the years I have met many talented artists/designers like Mark Ouellette, David Simpson, and Steve Skutka who were generous in sharing their techniques and knowledge with me. Without them, I'd probably still be creating dolls with three foot frizzed Afros!

This doll was created in memory of Mark Ouellette.

Creations by
JIM FARAONE

As all the artists and designers featured in this book, my designs and techniques are always evolving. With each passing day, I try something new and experiment quite a bit, it keeps my line of outfits fresh, so I don't get caught up in the repetition of creating the same look over and over.

Designing and creating is fun, so pick up that fabric, needle and thread and sew yourself into oblivion!

JEAN HASKETT

As long as I can remember, I enjoyed making costumes for paper dolls. In those days you could buy a book for ten cents, usually of some movie star. I would trace the doll, then build the costume and fill in the colors with crayons. I spent hours and hours and loved it.

My interest in dolls was limited. I had a Betsy Wetsy and that was about it. Of course, the BARBIE® doll was nowhere to be found.

After graduating, I decided I wanted a career in costume design and attended Frank Wiggins Trade School (which later became a college) in Los Angeles. I met very interesting and talented people and began to see what the fashion world was really like. That was definitely a period of growth toward the basic construction of design for me.

About that time Cupid stepped in and altered my path substantially. It wasn't until the early '60s when my girls became interested in "grown up" dolls, that we found our girl, the BARBIE® doll. My mother and I promptly made gobs of clothes for her and once in a while bought an outfit we thought was "neat". Of course, as little girls do - they soon felt the BARBIE® doll was much too childish and went on to other pursuits. Thus she was put away until one day when I decided it was time to clean out the "toys" of childhood and came across their dolls and outfits. My interest was sparked again and I decided to see just where she was. Well, what a surprise! She had multiplied many times over and so gorgeous!! Of course I had to have everyone I could see. Soon I began planning outfits and gathering materials. I had a neighbor who was interested in Kewpie dolls and she and I both wanted to find a BARBIE® doll club and more information about our new found interests. At a Kewpie doll luncheon we were given the name of a lady who was interested in starting a club, thus our Golden State BARBIE® Doll Club was born. Of course, being involved in a club only encouraged my desire to plan and make

costumes for the BARBIE® doll, which I have been doing since 1982. My interest lies mostly with Historical or Futuristic costumes and especially Ethnic costumes. Dolls have told the fashion story for centuries, and the BARBIE® doll is certainly the perfect model for such.

Although I only make six to eight outfits a year for the BARBIE® and Ken® doll, I enjoy every stitch. I am fascinated with leather which is my favorite material to work with. Along with the leather came my interest in Native Americans and the Wild West scene.

> **Jean Haskett**
> **2032 E. Shamwood St.**
> **West Covina, CA. 91791-1522**

> Outfit made from a
> pair of gloves.

Photos by Eric Lucas.

Creations by
Jean Haskett

Shaka Chief of
the Zulu

Elizabeth R.

Apache
Maiden.

King of Siam
& Salome
(Rita
Hayworth).

BRUCE A. NYGREN

My association with the BARBIE® doll began at a very young age. My sisters had a BARBIE® doll, along with Midge, Skipper® and Ken® dolls, so I designed and made outfits for their dolls. My mother had a sewing room that was designed especially for her with a hip height cutting table. I can still recall standing under it and watching the fabric scraps fall to the floor, anticipating which ones would be mine. My appreciation of beautiful fabrics has been life long.

In 1977 I received my Master's Degree in Textile design. I then designed wall tapestries for a few years. When a customer of mine wanted a coat made out of fabric like the tapestry I had woven for her home, I started designing clothes. This led to the opening of my designer boutique in Idyllwild, California. In that store loft I wove fabric and designed a line of women's clothes for many years.

I began designing for the BARBIE® doll again after my niece, Amy Aurora Nygren, was born in September 1988. For Christmas I gave her a BARBIE® doll. Then I started to shop for outfits for Amy's doll. Being a textile designer, I was disappointed in the fabrics that were used in the manufactured clothes. I always saved scraps, so, I bought some patterns and started making Amy some BARBIE® doll clothes. Some of the dresses were beaded by hand and were a big hit. My sister-in-law told me that people were trying to steal Amy's doll clothes.

Soon after this I read a short paragraph about a BARBIE® doll show in Pomono. I went to see what it was all about. When I asked why there was no one doing original clothes for the BARBIE® doll, I was told that no one would buy it if it didn't have a company stamp on it. This was six years ago.

I decided to try selling my creations at a BARBIE® doll show put on by the Inland Empire BARBIE® Doll Club with the encouragement of Faye Quiroz. At the first show, I presented my outfits in boxes that I had designed with a clear acrylic window. I had

brought thirty-six outfits in boxes and several on "fit models", whose hair had been done by Peter Nickel. Peter has had no formal training as a hair designer but has much experience playing with the BARBIE® doll's hair as a child. His love for the doll and his creative flair for styling the hair continues.

My designs have evolved dramatically since the first show. Twice a year I shop in New York for fabrics and beads. In 1994 I traveled to Milan in search of materials. All of the jewelry for the dolls is designed by my mother, Betty Bishop. She uses Austrian crystals and semi-precious stones like the ones she uses in her line of women's jewelry.

Most people think that I'm a BARBIE® doll collector. I'm not, but I do collect other things including hand blown and fused glass, masks from around the world, and of course, textiles.

I believe I have been blessed, because there has never been a time in my life when the creative ideas have not flowed abundantly. I love designing for the BARBIE® doll, buying fabrics for them, and designing each one as an original. As long as there are collectors who enjoy my work, I will continue to create.

Bruce A. Nygren
7882 McDowell Dr.
Las Vegas, NV. 89129

KAYANDEM

I am always uncomfortable trying to write a bio on us. It's such a weird topic - our attraction to the BARBIE® doll. I sometimes just don't get it! Anyway here goes.

When I was eight I would go over to my friend Robert Emmett's and while he was watching football I would be on the front steps with his sisters dressing their BARBIE® dolls. This was 1970 and I don't remember the dolls or the clothes, but I knew I was having fun.

Karlos' first memory is of Ava the girl down the street. Every week she would get a new doll or outfit and all the other girls would gather in jealous anticipation, waiting to see what Ava got.

Years pass. Karlos is at a book launch/fashion show for Billy Boy. He comes home with a BARBIE® doll. Her hair gets teased and she is set upon the television.

Karlos Lucereo/Michael Surgey

In the beginning we take our ideas of what is happening in fashion today and brainstorm a group of clothes. Karlos will sketch them out and we then decide which ones we like and Karlos does the patterns. After Karlos sews a sample we discuss and make alterations. When the patterns are finalized I take them and our previous patterns and sit in a pile of fabric. I then separate into little groups fabrics and textures that work together. From there I start going through the patterns designing outfits matching the right fabrics to the right patterns. After the group is on paper with fabric swatches, I start cutting it. It is then put in the sewing box where Karlos will get it. When finished it is returned to me for the finishing touches - snaps, beads, hooks, etc. At this point I go to a large supply of dolls and find the right one for the outfit, usually basing it on eye and hair color. If it is to be a mold-head doll I start mixing paints

More time passes. It is December 1991, Trisha and Francesca bring two BARBIE® dolls to a birthday party. We are there. They have stockings on (the BARBIE® dolls). We hold them and we are hooked. I think it is as it happened in the beginning. The realness of the BARBIE® doll and that fantastic element of style and fashion caught us.

The BARBIE® doll has come a long way over the years and somewhere along the way lost some of her fashion sense. I guess Kayandem was born out of our desire for a return to that.

We did our first BARBIE® doll show in October of 1993 and have found our way, albeit on the fringe, in this crazy world of BARBIE® doll collecting. Who would have thought! And who would have known how far spread and wonderful the people could be. And on top of that who would have known how much time and hard work would be involved. I don't think this was in our "what I want to be when I grow up" plans.

I would like to explain how we do it at Kayandem. First off, what the hell...oops I mean, what does Kayandem mean? My name is Michael Surgey, I am the em. My partner is Karlos Lucereo, he is the Kay. In other words K&M! O.K. now what do each of us do? Most people assume that one of us does the hair and one does the clothes. It's not that simple. We both have our separate talents, but they overlap in many ways.

to get the right color. If it is to be a reroot, I sigh and prepare myself for many hours of work. And if I am just going to work with the original hair I start boiling the water. The doll is then dressed. I then make the jewelry, and if she is to have eyelashes she goes back to Karlos for some serious surgery.

Now that scenerio is on a good day. Many times pieces are recut or resewn, or sometimes just scrapped. Quite often an original hair doll becomes a mold head. Sometimes nasty language is heard. And once in awhile you might find a BARBIE® doll flying through the air.

Finally they are tagged,

Kayandem
518 Crane Blvd., Los Angeles, CA. 90065

named, photographed, and boxed.

Luckily Karlos and I have the same sensibilities. We like trends and color and things a little odd. We hope that a Kayandem doll in someone's collection stands out and is special. And we want a reaction! Even if it is a look of horror we know we are doing something right. The BARBIE® doll jumped out and caught us. That is what we want our dolls to do.

There it is. A little about us. It is amazing that the BARBIE® doll has become such a big part of our lives. We look forward to seeing where she takes us this year as we start traveling more. It's a wild ride, who could ask for anything more?

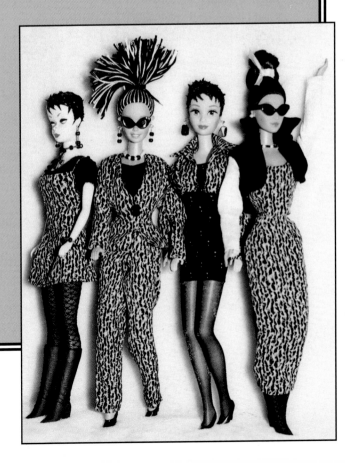

I never met a doll I didn't like - literally. I about had them all but the BARBIE® doll was, well, very special.

When I got my first #1 BARBIE® doll, I was 12 years old. I can still remember my mother's words to me when I begged for an extra $3.00, an advance on my allowance, to buy this gorgeous doll. "You're getting a little old for dolls, aren't you?"

I explained to her that this wasn't a baby doll or just a play doll. She was special. Even then, I had this instinct about her being more than just a doll.

So, I did get that doll and several of the now-very-expensive fashions such as "Roman Holiday", "Easter Parade" and even "Gay Parisienne". I remember being fascinated with the fine sewing details and the accessories!

I had grown up sewing by hand for all my dolls: Tiny Tears, Madame Alexander's - Cissy, especially, and others. Naturally I started "designing" clothes for the BARBIE® doll, almost all of which I sewed by hand at first because we didn't have a sewing machine until I was about 14. It got to be such a big deal with my girlfriends and me that we'd get together with an older lady in the neighborhood (she was probably about my age now, and I thought she was old!) and design BARBIE® doll clothes. I would usually take the lead because all these ideas would pop into my head.

As it turns out, the older lady had an extensive art background and often we'd sketch some designs first. Sometimes, I'd drape fabrics to see how they'd look. We did everything. It was a regular New York City design studio in the desert (El Paso, Texas).

My girlfriends and I didn't really play with the BARBIE® doll. We designed and did fashion shows, complete with runways, stages, etc.

Over the years, I studied art and always wanted to go to New York and be a fashion designer. However, it wasn't in the cards.

Like many girls my age, I went away to college, not New York, got a degree in business but still studied art, fashion design, and arts and crafts whenever I'd hear about a class or see something that interested me.

When my daughter was old enough for a BARBIE® doll, we dabbed in designs for her dolls; and eventually after being away from my vintage BARBIE® dolls for these intervening years, I accidentally came upon a #3 BARBIE® doll with a severe hair cut at a garage sale and the rebirth of a BARBIE® doll fanatic and amateur fashion designer happened.

Over the last several years, the hobby has evolved into a business and I have incorporated my zest for fashion design and my love of arts and crafts and painting into making outfits and accessories for the BARBIE® doll.

A friend once asked me to make her a "Gay Parisienne" and we searched for the "Perfect Fabric", found something close and I haven't looked back since. Designing dozens if not hundreds of my own, the BARBIE® doll has kept me busy.

I make almost all of my own accessories, from custom wide-brimmed straw hats and purses to poodles for the BARBIE® doll to be displayed with. I even make the leash, collar, and dog tag. All of the doll's poodles are named Fifi (the ones I do), but if a customer wants a name that will fit on a tag about the size of a very small flattened pea, then the name is changed to something very short!

I can do just about anything. My preference is the styles from the '60s, but I do incorporate some of the '40s, '50s and even today's styles into my original designs.

My favorite BARBIE® dolls are the vintage '60s era. There is just something so classic and reminiscent about the BARBIE® doll during this era, that it will always be my favorite.

Often I do limited editions, one-of-a-kind and even custom made designs. One customer sends sketches and photos from old fashion magazines, etc. and I design a fashion very similar to the sketch or photo for her.

One of my favorite aspects of designing for the BARBIE® doll is the creation of the accessories since I love to create and paint. I seldom use a pattern for my accessories so each will vary slightly from the next. Most of my jewelry is hand-made by me but there is some very nice pre-made jewelry on the market that I will use occa-

Check It Out.

Jonell Belke
Just Her Style
445 Dillard Lane
Coppell, TX. 75019

Creations by
JONELL BELKE

sionally. I make most of my own gloves because there is a shortage out there and colors and lengths are limited. I like to make a mid-length glove for some fashions (about 1/2 way between the wrist and the elbow). This is a very appealing look for me, possibly influenced by the beautiful clothes and accessories, especially gloves, my mother had in the late '40s and into the '50s.

One thing about designing for the BARBIE® doll, is that she never complains about being stuck with a pin (I fit each and every fashion to a #4 BARBIE®), she looks good in anything from sophisticated to almost tacky (as in my "Barbie doll on Tour", VERY colorful outfit), and...she NEVER gains weight. So I don't have to adjust my designs for any changes to her figure. She's always beautiful, always alluring, and ready for just about anything I can dream up!

In the last year, I have started creating celebrity (such as Jackie Kennedy dolls and fashions) and many designer dolls that have totally re-done facial paint, many are re-rooted, or at the very least, have restyled hair. I've also added mix-and-match fashions and accessories to my line. Typically, I will do a fashion that has a jacket and mink or fur stole, several pairs of gloves, etc. and the fashion can then be worn with the stole, the jacket, or both. Often, I like to display dolls with these fashions holding or trailing the mink stole or coat as a model would when she's modeling a fashion.

"Royalty", re-styled hair, repaint, and mink stole.

Creations by
JONELL BELKE

My accessory packs often include a purse, scarf, shoes, hat, and gloves. There are many variations and original designs.

Designing for the BARBIE® doll has been and I hope will always stand for creativity, fun, and friendship. I consider designing for the BARBIE® doll an art form and enjoy it tremendously and especially like bringing that enjoyment to my friends and customers.

Platinum re-root, re-paint.

"Jackie"

"Lady Bug, Lady Bug."

AILEEN RAYBON

I have been sewing for the BARBIE® doll since 1961, making my own patterns. I sewed for my 1961 BARBIE® doll and for my nieces' dolls. I still have my original doll and the box she came in. I started sewing for the public in 1989 when I sent an ad to a BARBIE® doll magazine.

My business in patterns and ready made outfits has grown beyond anything I could imagine. I love creating new outfits for the BARBIE® doll but I stay behind with my sewing.

I have designed outfits for "Phantom of the Opera", "Gone With The Wind", "Breakfast

Dorothy Aileen Raybon with some of her ladies.

at Tiffany's", Marilyn Monroe, Mae West, wedding gowns for brides to use on their tables, costumes for designers, and many other outfits.

I am a retired art teacher. I taught in Texas then we moved to Alabama and I taught eight years here.

I have three catalogues on my patterns: Book 1 has 100 patterns, whereas Books 2 and 3 have 50 patterns each. These pattern books are for sale through me.

Aileen Raybon
Aileen's Petite Fashions
829 Fort Dale Rd.
Greenville, AL. 36037

"Phantom of the Opera" created for Katherine Reynolds of Ohio.

Creations by
AILEEN RAYBON

A reproduction of a dress worn by Marilyn Monroe in *Gentleman Prefer Blonds*.

Various reproduction costumes I have created.

DEBBIE LUSTMAN

My love of the BARBIE® doll started many years ago. Since I was born in 1958, (and was always mature for my age) I'm sure I would have really appreciated a #1 BARBIE® doll at the age of three months. My parents, however, didn't see it that way. I had to wait until I was six, when my Godparents bought me a blonde bubble cut, a blonde Skipper® doll, and a Skipper® doll case. Boy, did I love those dolls - until the twist-n-turn BARBIE® doll came out and I rushed to Kiddie City toy store to trade in that "ugly doll" for the new model.

Although we always had plenty of BARBIE® dolls, mom really didn't want to pay all of that money for authentic

Debbie Lustman and her husband, Steve.

BARBIE® doll clothes, so we made them ourselves. I even made clothes for my Liddle Kiddles. Luckily, I had a friend named Tina (who was an only child and had everything) so I got to see and copy the type of stuff Mattel made. I often even traded my homemade clothes for authentic BARBIE® doll clothes. I've often wondered what the moms of the neighborhood thought of that!

As I grew older my dolls lived by themselves in the basement. I had no interest in them, but couldn't bear to part with them. Unfortunately, my brother-in-law threw them out while cleaning the basement one day.

I rediscovered the BARBIE® doll in 1987, and naturally it

wasn't long before I was at the fabric stores, dreaming about the beautiful outfits I wanted to make for my new dolls.

The more I design for the BARBIE® doll, the more I realize that she lends herself well to all styles. I try to make a wide variety of outfits - dresses, gowns, pants, mod stuff - I like to experiment with it all. Many times a fabric "speaks" to me, telling me exactly what to do with it. One of my favorite parts of redesigning a doll is making the jewelry. I love to find just the right crystals, beads, or chain to compliment my clothing designs.

After all, an outfit isn't complete until it's perfectly accessorized!

Debbie Lustman
324 W. Lincoln Ave.
Magnolia, N.J. 08049-1163

Creations by
DEBBIE LUSTMAN

JAMES BOGUE

The look of Bogue's Vogues is based on 1950s glamour in everything from casual daytime to striking evening wear.

I'm a native Texan and before deciding on a career in cosmetology, I found creative outlets in jobs such as department store display and working for a dressmaker. About the time I started collecting the BARBIE® doll, I was working for a dressmaker - it didn't take long for me to see that real clothes were not for me. I began developing my line of 11-1/2 inch couture in the early '80s, but I've been a fan of the BARBIE® doll since childhood.

What began as a hobby has become a lucrative business as more and more collectors across the country are discovering the glamour of Bogue's Vogues.

Attending the 1990 Dallas BARBIE® doll convention, I took some of my creations to the salesroom. I was absolutely ecstatic that people were buying my designs.

From there I went on to do local doll shows, and finally an ever growing mail-order business. Mail order allows me to reach the widest possible audience.

Noted in newspapers and magazine articles, Bogue's Vogues have been showcased in galleries, featured at conventions, and have won blue ribbons in competition. In a recent feature in a BARBIE® doll magazine it describes Bogue's Vogues as "stunningly simple" and a "marvel of workmanship".

I strive to use fine fabrics and impeccable fit to enhance the classic lines of my nostalgic creations. Some favorite inspirations for Bogue's Vogues come from such greats as Charles James, Edith Head, and naturally Lucy Ricardo. Inspiration is also drawn from vintage films and fashion magazines and of course, the BARBIE® doll's early wardrobe.

One of my table centerpiece dolls for a BARBIE® doll convention was dressed in Lana Turner's coat, a tribute to one of my favorite movies, *Imitation of Life*.

It's great to be a part of this aspect of BARBIE® doll collecting. With all the artists doing such beautiful and varied looks there's sure to be something for everyone.

Creating Bogue's Vogues is truly a labor of love and provides endless opportunities for self-expression.

James Bogue
Bogue's Vogues
4216 Geddes Ave.
Fort Worth, TX. 76107

Photos by Jeff Nestor.

Photos by Jeff Nestor.

ANN MEILI

I was born in Philadelphia, Pennsylvania and was the youngest of three children. I was raised in southern New Jersey in Haddon Heights and Cherry Hill.

I attended college in New Jersey and California studying Human Resources Management and aviation.

In 1985 I married a United Airlines captain at a private ceremony in San Carlos, California.

I started as a flight attendant for Piedmont Airlines in the late 1960s. In the early and mid '70s I was a corporate flight attendant flying celebrities on a private owned aircraft. Continuing my career in the airlines I worked for World Airways in Chicago and Newark. After leaving World, I also left the United States and moved to Amman, Jordan where I was a flight attendant for the Royal Jordanian Airlines flying throughout Europe, the Middle East, and Asia. From Jordan I relocated back to Cherry Hill, New Jersey and began flying for Global International Airways, a Kansas City based charter airline. I stopped flying in the 1980s and am looking forward to going back to the skies in 1996.

I became interested in the BARBIE® doll when a dear friend met Sandi Holder...he then introduced me to the wonderful world of the BARBIE® doll. I started slow as I was unsure what I was involved in and I am sure that I made many mistakes as a neophyte dealer. I taught myself to reroot through trial and error. Once I felt comfortable rerooting, Rob Baiz and I started rerooting and painting newer dolls and marketing them. After Rob died, I needed a new person to help with the painting and I asked Linda Ladd of Lombard, Illinois to help. Linda and I then began offering custom dolls, rerooting and repainting vintage dolls for collectors. As I got busier it was necessary to add another person to our duet, so in 1995 Laura Jicha of Sylmar, California joined our team. Now this trio reroots, repaints, and repairs vintage dolls. Additionally, we offer custom dolls by special order. I do all the rerooting, Linda and I sew, and Laura and Linda paint. Laura is capable of repairing neck splits, pin pricks, nose nicks, and broken fingers.

Robin Quivers of Howard Stern fame has a doll that was specially ordered for her by an ABC affiliate. ABC weatherman Randy Rauch has a doll that was created for him. Katey Segal of "Married With Children" has a Peg Bundy look alike. Bob Mackie has a rerooted Ken® doll with long frosted hair. All of these dolls were created by one or all of us for these celebrities.

Ann Meili
7345 Palmyra Ave.
Las Vegas, NV. 89117

Creations by
ANN MEILI

Photos by Cindy Kent.

PABBOO GERONIMO REDFEATHER

My love affair with the BARBIE® doll began at age five. My mother's friend brought a box full of toys for us to have. As my mom's friend spread out the toys on the table, I was fascinated with the BARBIE® doll. She was a dark brown BARBIE® doll wearing the "Career Girl" outfit. As I got older, I kept dreaming of this doll my mom took away from me and gave to my sister. The BARBIE® doll is a little person and most children are amazed at little people.

I was born in New Rochelle, New York and both my parents are artistic. My father draws landscapes and my mother is an interior decorator. I come from a rich background, my mother is a Native American and my father is Black and Native American mix. All my brothers and sister are artistic. I was the only one who dived into it. At age 15, I had oil paintings that toured America as part of a Native American student display. I received a special diploma for Basic Art.

I remember watching mom sew us clothes and make dresses. I was fascinated with old movies like Shirley Temple films and *The Wizard of Oz* with Glinda the Good Witch.

At age 21, I made my first BARBIE® doll dress. It was blue, white, and pink. I still have the dress to this day.

My mother had long black hair and I would comb it and curl it. She one day told me to cut it, and so I did and it turned out really nice. My mom later encouraged me to go to beauty school and I got a degree in cosmetology.

My cousin was a runway model and she asked me to do her hair a few times. I was fascinated with the modeling business. I later worked in the fashion business doing hair which was a lot of fun.

Keeping my creative juices flowing, I entered costume competitions with people who are in the industry. I won three years in a row. What an honor competing against professionals and winning!

The first BARBIE® convention I went to was the 25th Anniversary in New York. I spent time with Kitty Black Perkins in the competition room. She asked me a lot of questions. I also attended the 30th Anniversary convention and the BARBIE® doll Festival in Florida. I was happy to be involved with BARBIE® doll friends and I am credited with putting on the first Black BARBIE® doll, Hispanic BARBIE® doll and Tropical BARBIE® doll party. All the parties were successful and a great deal of fun. I have been on the news four times because of the BARBIE® doll: a talk show, a radio show, and interviewed by Mattel.

The BARBIE® doll has taken me to many exciting places where I have made the nicest friends.

I love designing one-of-a-kind creations for the BARBIE® doll and hope to share my creations for others to enjoy.

Long live the Queen — BARBIE® doll!

Pabboo Geronimo Redfeather
14641 Delano #9
Van Nuys, CA. 91411

Creations by
PABBOO GERONIMO REDFEATHER

PAUL CREES/PETER COE

We have been professional doll artists since 1979 and are well known on the International "Doll Art" scene. Our dolls have been nominated for awards of excellence by *DOLLS* magazine and our work is regularly featured in specialist doll journals in France, Germany, England, Australia, Japan, and the U.S.A.!

We see the world as a stage and devote our lives to creating portraits celebrating its players. Many admirers believe we have coaxed the art of wax portraiture into a new realm. They have compared our creations with such legendary Victorian artists as Pierotti, Marsh, and Montanari.

In Paris, France in 1994, we won the coveted Jumeau Award for our entire "body of work" at the World Congress of Dolls.

Our editions are small (never more than fifty and usually only ten to twenty pieces). We have created lifelike interpretations of Vivien Leigh, Barbra Streisand, and Elizabeth Taylor.

Paul states, "As a young man I loved art and fashion, which led me to my first job as a costume assistant on the musical version of "Gone With The Wind" in London's West End. After a few other stints, I began working for Britain's oldest repertory theater, the Old Vic, where my knowledge of costuming greatly benefited from the theater's multifaceted productions. While working in the theater I began experimenting with doll making by sculpting a head of Marlene Dietrich, then began making replicas of Dietrich and dressing them in costumes from her most celebrated films. Since I collect and have a large collection of Marlene Dietrich memorabilia, it was a natural progression for me. From Dietrich I went on to Garbo and the rest is history."

While at the Bristol Old Vic, I met Peter, whose background in costume design matched my own. Discovering we were kindred spirits, in 1980 we became a team.

Today we both jointly undertake the sculpting. I model and paint most of the heads, while Peter concentrates on the difficult task of wax pouring and doll construction. We both sculpt the hands and legs.

We agree that one of the most enjoyable parts of the process is deciding who will be the next subject. After much give-and-take before settling on a person, we study countless photos, books, and videos.

When we entered the field of poured-wax dolls, we found little research available and very few artists working in the medium. We were self-taught and have succeeded in keeping alive an age-old tradition of doll making that was in danger of disappearing.

"We have never collected dolls, though I have developed a passionate interest in doll houses and miniatures," says Paul. "However, in 1993 I purchased my first BARBIE® doll and as many BARBIE® doll fanatics will appreciate, the one very quickly became several, which has naturally led to a BARBIE® doll collecting mania that some would describe as panic buying."

Peter is a little more restrained, buying in small multiples of six.

We appreciate the glamorous appeal and the design concept that embraces the BARBIE® doll ethos.

"In addition to collecting the BARBIE® doll, I have developed an interest in the '70s concept fashion doll Darci® and her companions," states Paul.

Dressing the BARBIE® doll is an entirely new department for us, but we are excited about the artistic opportunities that lie ahead.

Paul Crees/Peter Coe
The Paul Crees Collection
124 Alma Rd.
Bournemouth BH9 1AL
Dorset, England

Creations by
PAUL CREES/PETER COE

ANTHONY FERRARA

It's thrilling to see my designs on superstars like Whitney Houston, Cher, Tina Turner, Barbra Streisand, Diana Ross, Cheryl Tiegs, Brook Sheilds, Pia Zadora, Venessa Redgrave, Barbara Mandrell, Linda Evans, Rita Moreno, and more. Or to pick up a copy of *Cosmopolitan, Vogue*, and *Harper's Bazaar* and find one of my belts or handbags in a fashion layout.

The 11-1/2 inch dolls are my favorite clients because they don't talk back and they never change sizes.

I have been designing clothes for over thirty years and during the past nineteen years I have received recognition as the preeminent designer of mesh clothing. The metallic mesh is expensive due to the manufacturing and the time-consuming procedures needed to create wearable apparel.

My 11-1/2 inch dolls made their BARBIE® doll convention debut in Birmingham, Alabama, represented by Howell Scott. All my dolls are one-of-a-kind as each has its own distinct flair and as collectors say, "Are stunning beauties".

I graduated from the Boston School of Fashion Design and studied costume tailoring in Italy. After establishing a couture shop in the United States, I began experimenting with a variety of unique trim for my fashions, including metal mesh. At first I bought mesh handbags and cut them up. Eventually I discovered the source of the material in Massachusetts.

My BARBIE® doll fashions wear many variations of mesh. Mesh cannot be sewn in the traditional sense. Each dot has four legs which have to be opened with another dot slipped through and then closed.

I began making mesh costumes for fashion dolls about sixteen years ago. Originally the mesh was made only in gold and silver. With my encouragement for designing, today there are many new finishes and color combinations. Even experimenting with hologram on the mesh. These dolls were made as gifts for special events and occasions.

The first commercial fashion doll to wear my shimmering mesh is a design for Louis Nichole. The doll was the $6,000 Marilyn Monroe.

I have no plans to mass produce the mesh clothing fashion dolls. The mesh is much more expensive than most doll fabric. Also it's a challenge to work on such small figures. The accessories require demanding skill, particularly the mesh handbags, belts, and jewelry. So my dolls must remain a very limited edition.

The facial painting and coiffures of the dolls have been glamorized by Howell Scott, and my wife, Rose.

Anthony Ferrara
c/o Howell Scott
2429 Chuchura Dr.
Birmingham, AL. 32544

Photos by Judith Whorton.

Some of my career highlights are:

• Prepared product presentations for international designers - Gianni Versace, Missoni, Emanuell Kahn, Paco Roban, and Zhandra Rhodes.

• In 1990 I was commissioned to create an exclusive fashion for the famous Absolut Vodka ad campaign; the same campaign which previously featured the art of Andy Warhol and Keith Haring, the fashions of Marc Jacobs and David Cameron. The new ad, Absolut Ferrara showcased a shimmering silver mesh dress and turban.

• Although no other apparel designer had been invited to create more than one garment, Absolut requested another one-of-a-kind dress from me - an 18 karat gold Absolut Fashion. This $500,000 dress was photographed for the cover of Absolut's pull-out ad in *Vogue* magazine.

• I was the guest designer at the Miami Apparel Mart.

• A two-time guest designer at Atlanta Apparel Mart.

• I've made guest appearances on numerous talk shows and television magazine programs.

• The first designer to utilize mesh fabric in commercially successful apparel.

One of the advantages of mesh fabric is that it is so durable. These dolls will remain as shimmering and dazzling 100 years from now. A thing of beauty is a joy forever.

Photo by Judith Whorton.

Silver Lining

Photo by Judith Whorton.

Photos by Judith Whorton.

HOWELL SCOTT

With Anthony Ferrara'a busy schedule, I handle the sales of his wonderful creations.

I began my BARBIE® doll collection eleven years ago. In this amount of time, I have filled three rooms with BARBIE® dolls and am working on the fourth.

My husband finds a place for all of them. In some of the rooms, the dolls line the walls from ceiling to floor. There are also showcases filled with a variety of doll treasures, from antique bisque dolls to the latest in the Mattel line.

I love BARBIE® because of her exquisite sense of fashion. Studying her fashions from 1959 until today is a real lesson in fashion history.

I'm a fur consultant for a leading department store chain and have worked as a fashion model and even hosted my own radio show. I have also taught courses at several business colleges.

I enjoy the new friends I have made through collecting. My first BARBIE® doll convention was in Omaha, Nebraska in 1991 and I haven't missed one since. They are like a giant family reunion.

My BARBIE® doll collection ranges from vintage dolls and fashions to the BARBIE® doll dressed by high fashion designers. Of course I favor the well known designer, Anthony Ferrara, who costumes his BARBIE® dolls in glittering metallic fashions. I now restyle the doll's hair and apply makeup to go with the elegant shimmering fashions that are Anthony's fashion trademark.

My doll collection numbers about 3,000 and it's difficult to say which is my favorite doll. Although, my favorite fashion is Mattel's "Enchanted Evening".

I don't buy dolls for investment - I collect them for the pleasure they give me. In stressful times I just go to work with the BARBIE® dolls. It's amazing how one's attitude changes after a few hours with my hobby. I love the BARBIE® doll because just like a good friend, she enriches my life.

Howell Scott
2429 Chuchura Dr.
Birmingham, AL. 32544

Photos by Judith Whorton.

Creations by
HOWELL SCOTT

Pink Champagne

Gold Rush

Blue Ice

Photos by Judith Whorton.

SUZY SEASE

My fascination with BARBIE® started at age four, when much to my delight I received my first BARBIE® doll. Since I was an only child I had quite an abundance of BARBIE® doll paraphernalia. There were fashions, structures, and every friend or family member produced.

At age twelve we moved from my childhood home. This prompted a huge cleaning of my toys and BARBIE® dolls. Much of the items were given to the children of family friends. Of course this kind of gesture now disheartens me as much of those give-aways are hard to find collectibles!

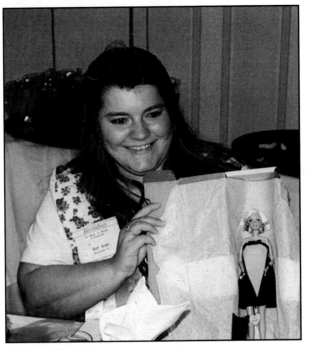

After the move, boys replaced the BARBIE® doll. I met a guy who had a connecting paper route to mine. After years of hit and miss, perfect timing prevailed. A nine year crush was ended and we were married. We both have an interest of old cars and both drove Mustangs as our first cars. He started restoration on my "66" Mustang a week after we started dating. This prompted me to start my own hobby. After an attic search there were about six dolls and a few outfits, one of which was my first BARBIE® doll. She is in much loved condition but a treasured start to a new adventure. I combined my talents of crafts with my BARBIE® doll hobby. This evolved into painting jackets, tote bags, chairs, and now making custom fashion doll furniture and creating dolls.

My husband Brian and I now take part in each others interest. We attend car and doll shows and even spot bargains for each other!

While doing my dolls I have four helpers to watch my every move. They are our pride and joy, which are three temperamental cats and a cocker spaniel named Shelby. Shelby is my constant shadow while the cats give an occasional visit between naps and play.

After thirteen years of collecting I have sold over half of my collection twice. This allows me to rule the collection rather than it rule me. After all this time I still find BARBIE® collecting a wonderful hobby which has brought me much happiness and several very special friends.

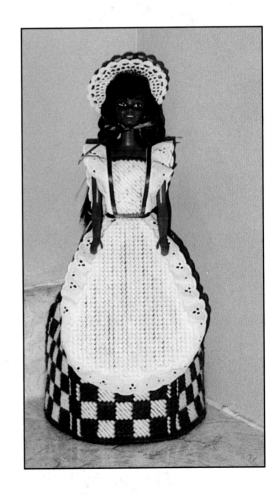

> **Suzy Sease**
> **804 Pine Grove Dr.**
> **Waynesboro, PA. 17268**

MARY FERRETTI

I am a native San Franciscan.

I received my first BARBIE® doll at the age of seven. She was a #4 BARBIE® doll and I fell in love with her. My mother was a seamstress. I had many fine fabrics at my disposal...and with that I was able to make all my BARBIE® doll's fashions...even her silk stockings! I made all of my clothing while in high school as well. I would never be caught wearing the same thing twice. That's probably where my "One-of-a-Kind" concept came from.

I attended school in San Francisco; San Francisco State University and the Academy of Art College.

I have worked in retail since I was 15; Sears, Liberty House, Joseph Magnin, and Macy's. My retail career entailed sales, assistant buyer, and fashion display/window visual merchandise presentation.

I was well known for my keen taste in fashion, my stylish hairstyles, and my color coordination in my mannequin presentation.

After the birth of my third child I made a career change. I knew I was great with fashion and mannequins...so, I took it one step further. The BARBIE® doll became my new mannequin...only in a miniature version.

I frequent fabric stores. I love silks, lace, satin, velvets, and appliqués. Each of my designs is a one-of-a-kind, "Work of Art". I fine detail the hair, makeup, jewelry, accessories, and

shoes with each garment. My dolls have to create a "complete fashion look" from head to toe. They are making a "statement".

All of us designers have a God given talent. We all have our own interpretation of what we would like the BARBIE® doll to look like. I'm glad we have the opportunity to share our interpretation with others and have them be seen and appreciated. I respect my fellow designers and I enjoy looking at their wonderful talents. I know what they put into their creations. Doll fashion designing is a world of its own. We are a group of artists involved with a fantasy motion picture actress and her private academy awards. I am proud to be a part of it.

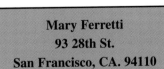

Mary Ferretti
93 28th St.
San Francisco, CA. 94110

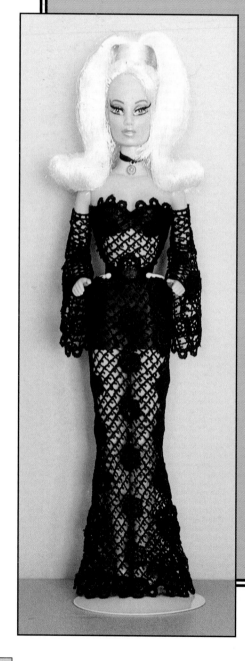

Creations by
MARY FERRETTI

That special something that the BARBIE® doll has has captured my heart since her (and my) early days in the '60s. I guess I am first an avid miniature collector because it was the tiny scale, detail, and accuracy of the doll's early accessories and wardrobe that first captured my attention and enthralled me. For me the BARBIE® doll was not just another fashion doll. She had this entire miniature world for me to escape to and entertain my fantasies. As a boy, I recall watching a lot of action/adventure shows on television. In turn, the BARBIE® doll had many action adventures such as earth-quakes and tornadoes which up ended everything. Then there was the fun of restoring everything to order. Many years later I gained expertise as a BARBIE® doll artist by restoring vintage dolls to their original beauty. Today I often strip a doll to her bare essentials by depilating her hair and removing all traces of facial paint. With a clean "canvas" I begin the time consuming process of hand rooting hair in another color, hand painting her face to reflect just the right expression, then design a custom couture ensemble with that special MiKelman touch. The result invariably is a stunningly beautiful, highly detailed, one-of-a-kind marvel.

MiKeLman
610 Blackwater Rd.
Chillicothe, OH. 45601

This 35th Anniversary BAR-BIE® doll was depilated and all facial paint was removed in order for me to remake the doll in a way that I felt more accurately captured the look of the #1 BARBIE® doll - with a twist - titian hair!

Creations by
MiKeLman

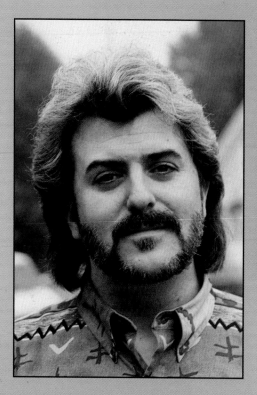

"Paul David, What a Doll!" A Jewel Secrets Ken® doll is rerooted, repainted, and reinterpreted to resemble Paul David.

This Fashion Jeans BARBIE® doll got the works: A reroot, totally new facial paint, and a MiKelman ensemble.

My "Lady Di" which sold for $1,000.

STEVEN TARANTO

I am a native of New England, to be exact Boston. This is where I learned how to work my skills into a trade. At the age of 14, I started my first apprenticeship with a master tailor in the garment district. Within eight months I found myself making a mature decision, with the help and support of my parents, that I wanted to take my passion and make it my career. Truly this is what happened.

I found myself wanting and needing to know everything about design. With the flood gates open, next came shoe design, hair, millinery, and last but not least jewelry. Suddenly I found myself with a small business that was doing rather well in small boutiques downtown. People I didn't know were requesting private commission pieces of all kinds. It was amazing! Like a snowball rolling down a hill, the business was growing faster and bigger than I could handle so I acquired a partner. Then it was onto bigger and better stores Fiorucci, Ellio. F., Saks Specialty Line, Nieman-Marcus New Trends Salon in Texas, Parachute of New York, Lord and Taylor Winter Specialty Line, The Forgotten Women, and Bloomingdale's Specialty Junior Line.

In the beginning it was fun, but as time went on and it got bigger, it became boring, routine, and draining. This time of my life was hard, fast and fun, but I was becoming burnt out. At Christmas that last year, a very close friend gave me a wonderful gift of a BARBIE® doll in a tub filled with what appeared to be bubbles looking very Marilyn. My love affair had begun. It was an absolute dream come true for an underworked imagination.

It also meant no more cost sheets and practical yardages. It was freedom! Freedom to stop when things weren't working and continuing when they were. Collecting at a frenzied pace, easy to keep up with at the time thankfully, I found myself buying outfits just for the shoes and then back to work. There from one end of the cutting table to the other she stood. The BARBIE® doll in all her glory. She wore recreations of my designs made to scale. Also Dior, Chanel, Charles James, Balmine, and even

Rudi Gernreich inspired outfits. There were no limits, no boundaries. Heaven!

Owners of a local toy store, whom I had known for years, had seen several of my dolls. They loved them and kept after me to start selling them. I wasn't sure if I wanted to sell or if they would sell. Finally I let them take two dolls and went on with my day. Five hours later the phone rang and to my surprise both dolls had sold and they were coming by for more.

With that, a new happier passion and career began. It's a truly wonderful feeling to be able to say I love my hobby which has become my work. It is my sincere wish that everyone can find a true blue friend and mentor as I have in both the BARBIE® doll and my friend Becky Asher.

Steven Taranto
39 Beacon St.
Chelsea, MA. 02150

Photos by Becky Asher.

Creations by
STEVEN TARANTO

Photos by Becky Asher.

Photos by Becky Asher.

BILL WALDOW

After 10 years of collecting BARBIE® dolls and family, new and vintage, I decided it was time for a change. Out came the sewing machine and that's where it started. The ideas and fashions would not stop coming. Casual, fancy, and sometimes a little far out, it was the most fun I had with the BARBIE® doll since starting to collect. Hairdos and jewelry followed, then make-up makeovers. It was really exciting showing my one-of-a-kind creations to friends and family. I then decided to make my dolls available to the public. After a slow start business picked up and each show brought more new customers. One of the best things about selling my dolls is seeing the repeat customers. I love seeing them at each show and it's nice to see people enjoying my creations as much as I enjoy creating them. My favorite dolls to work with are red heads and brunettes. I love the Nostalgic series and can't wait for the American Girl "Poodle Parade" doll to come out. The head molds I like to work with the most are the Steffie and Oriental (Miko) as they have a more sophisticated look. I always enjoy shopping for dolls to makeover as much as I do creating fashions, hairstyles, jewelry, etc. for them. I hope you enjoy them also.

Bill Waldow
1211 Vine St. #203
Denver, CO. 80206

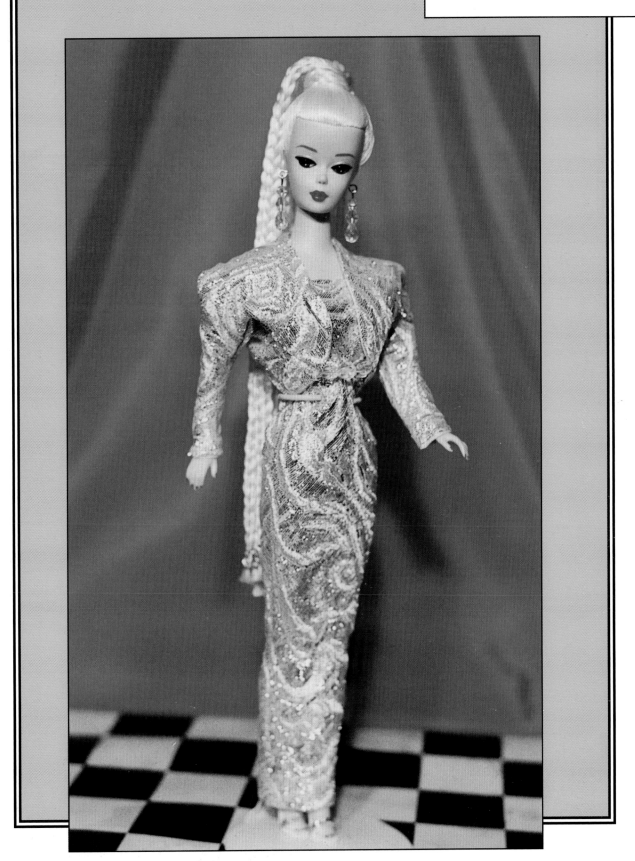

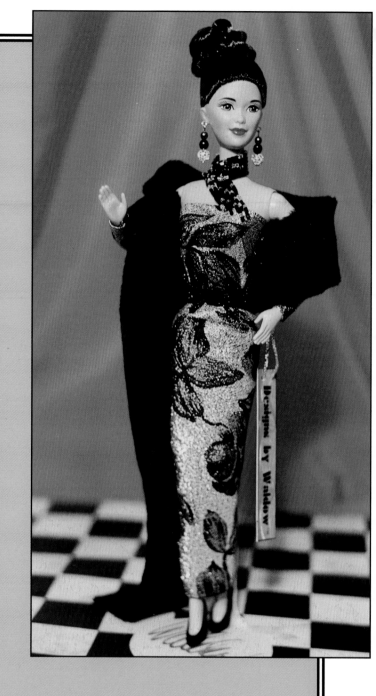

PATTE BURGESS

I enjoy designing glamourous haute couture, gala night, and fantasy fashions for the BARBIE® doll and other 11-1/2 inch fashion dolls. I work with a wide array of lavish fabrics, luxurious furs, and intricate jewelry.

Fashion design was my profession. I ran the "Copy Cat", a couture salon in Arcadia, California, for 10 years in the '60s and '70s. I employed fourteen seamstresses and was designing gowns for exclusive clientele.

I studied art at the University of Southern California and design at The Fashion Institute.

Design has always been an integral part of my life. I remember at the age of 7, taking my mother's sheer lilac curtains down to pin and drape a Grecian gown for myself. I was intent on expressing my individuality by making my own clothes.

After closing the "Copy Cat" I missed the creativity. I unpacked those trunks of baubles, beads, and fabrics which now adorn my new creations for the BARBIE® doll.

After a trip to Las Vegas, my granddaughter asked me what a Las Vegas showgirl was, so I decided to show her. I made several

showgirl costumes for her BARBIE® doll and a new vocation was born - Patte Burgess Designs.

My designs change frequently and I limit production to several dozen new additions. My garments are constructed without patterns, using the fabric to inspire the shapes.

My ensembles are sold separately, but for an additional fee I do include a doll. I redo the makeup and create a hairdo that will compliment the outfit.

Due to such tremendous response I am unable to accommodate the many requests for special custom orders. My husband Ken helps me out by making the boxes which hold my fashions.

This is not a money making adventure for me, but rather a way to appease my heart's desire to make beautiful clothing for the BARBIE® doll.

Patte Burgess
Patte Burgess Designs
444 Duarte Rd. H-1
Arcadia, CA. 91007

CHARLES L. MO

I developed an early awareness of quality clothing and the demands of construction and design that are characteristic of such quality. As a youth, I considered pursuing a fashion design or illustration career. I often spent leisure hours sketching designs in emulation of Givenchy, Chanel, Worth, James, and others. Yet, fate had other career directions and I became an art historian. Today, I work as Director of Collections and Exhibitions for the Mint Museum of Art in Charlotte, North Carolina.

My doll design work eventually came in response to my introduction to the world of collecting vintage BARBIE® dolls. I vaguely recall that such a fashion doll was available during my youth. It wasn't until 1989 that I was introduced to the quality craftsmanship that went into the design of the early BARBIE® dolls and related fashions. That introduction came about when I was offered a 1963 Bubble-cut BARBIE® doll to decorate my Christmas tree. I am a Christmas aficionado and always have a huge tree, frequently decorated with a theme. In 1989, the theme was vintage toys, dolls, and ornaments. I was immediately attracted to the quality of the Mattel garments - the tiny zipper and buttons, the miniature gloves, the wedge-style shoes and gleaming graduated pearl necklace! Within two weeks, I had purchased my first vintage BARBIE® doll – a Titian Bubble-cut doll. An introduction to BARBIE® dealers Lynn Blake and Joe Blitman helped me build an outstanding collection of over 200 vintage (1959-1971) dolls. I collect Mattel garments with a penchant for the 1600 series suits and formals as well as the more elaborate of the 900 clothing series. My passion for mint condition has led me to purchasing NRFB items and then opening them. My toy collecting interests extends to Ken® and Francie™ dolls, Miss Revlon dolls, Madame Alexander "Elise" dolls from the 1950s, and GI Joe®/Action Man figures from the 1960s and early 1970s.

Creating fashions for BARBIE® dolls revived youthful design desires. Working as an art museum director parallels many aspects of design, but doll fashion work has proven to be relaxing and rewarding for me. My designs are also inspired by the early Japanese production line which Mattel employed in the early years of the BARBIE® doll's existence. The designs which Charlotte Johnson pro-

duced for Mattel were incredible. In like manner, I love to discover elegant fabrics for use in my fashions. I design with the 1959-1965 BARBIE® dolls in mind. Vintage-based designs (often using vintage fabrics) for vintage-style fashion dolls.

Today, I continue my design work with original ensembles dressed on dolls I repaint and restyle thus creating my own distinct line of dressed dolls. Collectors appreciate the quality and craftsmanship I bring to each of my creations. I regularly present my artistry at doll shows around the country. As my products are

Charles L. Mo
406 Clarkson Green
Charlotte, NC. 28202

Photo of Charles L. Mo by David Ramsey.

one-of-a-kind creations, I prefer the doll show circuit to mail orders or catalogue lists. All in all, it's been most enjoyable for me. I've met so many wonderful people through my collecting and design work, that I believe doll collectors are among the best folks there are. Considering such, I thank the BARBIE® doll for bringing me into a common realm of interest with so many fine people. Many wonderful friendships have come about and for that, I am most appreciative.

STEVE SKUTKA

I was born in 1959, and started drawing by the age of 4 or 5. I always had a fascination for little worlds. Among my playthings were countless boxes made into houses or little worlds with clouds of cotton hung in the sky.

I was sewing by hand and machine by the age of 7. Now my little worlds were expanded by the construction of stuffed animals and cloth dolls. I even peddled my stuffed creatures to local neighbors.

The biggest creative drive I have was sparked by a mistake my father made. When I was very young I bought a paper doll book. This made my father furious and he took it from me and handed it to one of my sisters. I couldn't understand why I couldn't have dolls when they could. Now I was obsessed with them and had to have them.

After pestering my mother for years for my very own BAR-

BIE® doll, I was allowed to purchase one at the age of 10. However I was not allowed to buy any clothes. Hence my passion was born. If my doll was to have a wardrobe I would be creating it myself. I used store bought patterns at that time and was very unhappy with their "unMattel-like fit".

My work has concentrated on BARBIE® doll creations for the last 7 years, and has developed considerably in that time. I have won many awards for creative competition at conventions. I have also contributed to many conventions and designed dolls, like the Princess BARBIE® and Prince Ken®. Souvenir dolls for the 1991 Omaha convention. I am probably best known for my best of show creation "Starfleet BARBIE®".

I am currently attending the Fashion Institute of Technology for an Associates degree in Fashion Design, and a Bachelors in Toy Design.

Steve Skutka
48 Maple Ave.
Rockaway, N.J. 07866

Creations by
STEVE SKUTKA

JOSHARD ORIGINALS

JOE SEMINERIO/ JEFF BOUCHARD

Joshard Originals are the combined efforts of Jeff Bouchard and Joe Seminerio. Focusing our efforts on retro fashions from the '40s, '50s and early '60s. We have created some timeless beauties.

Bouchard has a degree in Art and Design and formerly worked as a buyer for Lord & Taylor and Brooks Brothers in New York City. His keen eye for design and detail can be seen in the masterful painting of the face makeup and finishing details of the outfit and jewelry.

Seminerio has been a hair designer for 21 years. After working in some of New York's exclusive salons and managing his own, he has found most of his time now dedicated to exquisite miniature coiffures. Seminerio has the talent to recreate any hairstyle from those days gone by. Dramatic upswept sausage curls, bubble bouffants, or a bouncy ponytail, a la Sandra Dee can be seen on a Joshard Original.

Along with the classic coiffures, our endless attention to the minute details, the carefully placed finishing curls around the face and the handcrafted jewelry all compliment our timeless fashion.

A cool, confident suit ensemble, smartly tailored or a romantic taffeta '40s inspired evening gown simply stating good taste and good manners, are the elements that inspire the Joshard design team to continue to pour our creative hearts into the 11-1/2 inch idol.

Joshard Originals
26 North 11th Street
Reading, PA 19601

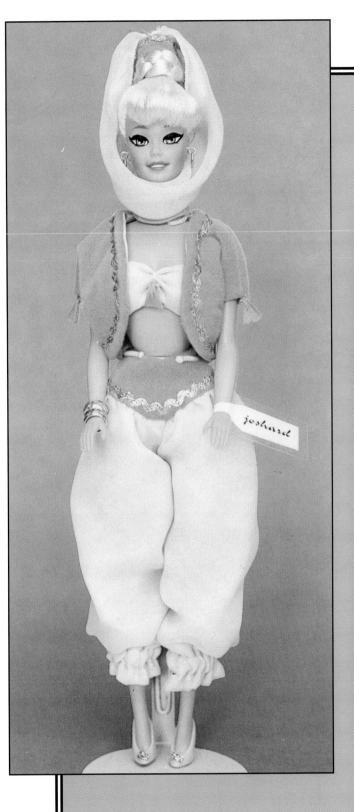

THE HOUSE OF CLOCHE

VALERIE LYN DAMOUR

I love God, and thank Him in all things always. I live in Saylorsburg, PA with my beloved family, my husband Lawrence Richard (Rick) Damour Jr. (who encourages me and helps me with everything), my two daughters Sara Lyn Damour, 18 and Brianne Lee Damour, 8 (who help me with the housework and give me their precious friendship), my son Matthew John Damour, 15 (who helped with the housework and delights me with his sports), my Bengal cat Raja (who consoles me when I'm tired),

Me in front of my life size 1964 BARBIE® doll kitchen.

my boxer Hootch (who watches out for me) and my conure, Pretty Bird (who sings for me). This is my family who cares for me and supports me in everything I do.

I grew up in the '60s. My favored play toy was the BARBIE® doll. I loved my dolls dearly and never went anywhere without them. I was heart broken when I was too old to really enjoy playing with them anymore and still remember my last attempt to play dolls with my friend. I took very good care of my doll outfits and had a great appreciation for the fine details of each outfit even then. I tried to sew some doll clothes back then and still have my early attempts. At the time I had all the desire but very little skill. I never dreamed I'd be fulfilling that desire 25 years later. Like most BARBIE® doll collectors, I rediscovered my old love, the BARBIE® doll, cleaning out my closet one afternoon. I hadn't seen my case of dolls and clothes in years. Right away I knew I had to have more of it etc., etc., etc... Well you know the rest. It's become a hobby/business my husband and I enjoy together. We even enjoy running two doll shows a year.

I get inspired by watching old movies of the '50s and '60s. Marilyn Monroe, Doris Day, Natalie Wood, Sandra Dee, Shelly

Fabres, and Elvis are some of my favorites. I also love the musicals of the same era. I have quite a collection of these vintage videos. I can appreciate all types of music, but my favorite music is the pop music of the '60s.

Putting together my outfits has become a real passion for me. They evolve slowly and not always in the direction you think they will. Now I enjoy my BARBIE® dolls just as much as I did when I was a child. I have always been fascinated with the BARBIE® doll's accessories and miniatures, so I get special satisfaction from designing pocketbooks, necklaces, gloves, hats, and other miniatures I include with each outfit.

The House of Cloche
P.O. Box 572
Wind Gap, PA. 18353

Designing Woman

I like to make my outfits in the tradition of the originals. I like to make them look authentic as possible by putting in lining, top stitching, snaps, zippers, and mother of pearl buttons. I look for fabrics that will do well making these tiny clothes. Some of these fabrics must be treated on all edges with a stop fray product because the pattern pieces are so small. I like to work in large numbers, cutting out 25-50 of the same outfit in one day. Or doing only hems and gathers. I want to make several hundred of each outfit so they will be limited, but also collectible. I package my outfits in Barbara Peterson's boxes for the completed vintage look. The outfits can be easily removed, by customers for display. Although I do not push religion on anyone, I include Biblical tracks with all my outfits because I want my customers to know that God cares and loves them.

My ads in BARBIE® doll magazines have brought me orders from across the country and around the world which include Puerto Rico, Austria,

Spin Drift

Early Bird

Creations by
THE HOUSE OF CLOCHE

Spring Dance

Australia, Japan, Switzerland, Germany, China, Finland, and Canada.

Today the world of the BARBIE® doll offers many wonderful things, but I like to remember the BARBIE® doll as that small town teenage girl.

I love the new nostalgic BARBIE® dolls. They offer loads of creative fun. I like to paint and reroot them, anything is possible. They make great models for vintage style outfits.

I have a collection from other BARBIE® doll artists such as Christoff Originals, MiKelman, Joshard, Debbie Lustman, and Ricky LaChance.

What does the future hold for the BARBIE® doll? I hope it's a series of vintage style BARBIE® doll movies done in the comedic style of vintage half hour TV shows! Will someone please tell Hollywood what the BARBIE® doll aficionados are missing?

Lemon Pucker

D.A.E. ORIGINALS

Have you ever been rummaging through some old boxes, looking for something and came across a childhood toy — a doll or a BARBIE® doll? Do you remember how much you loved her when she was first given to you? How about when you had finally saved enough allowance to buy her some new clothes or shoes? How, on top of all that, would you like to experience that feeling everyday?

The BARBIE® doll holds such a special place in the hearts of children and grown-ups alike. She varies from a few dollars to a few thousand. There is a market out there that few people are aware of. I'm going to call it "Barbieville". In "Barbieville" dreams are relived everyday. Men, women, and some children take the BARBIE® dolls that have been beaten and battered and turn them into magnificent dolls of art. D.A.E. Originals is one such company.

Specialty BARBIE® dolls are in high demand. Specialty stores and toy shops cannot keep collector dolls on the shelf. Large department stores carry BARBIE® doll "glamour", but a '90s version. Nothing from the days of old. D.A.E. Originals owners, Brian Schafer and David Escobedo recognized this and joined up to create what is known as "artistry" dolls.

In creating our masterpieces, we try to be as perfectly period correct as possible, trying not to create an anachronism. We specialize in historically correct time pieces, collectors, and childlike dolls that are made to look like their favorite movie and TV stars.

Time pieces take great time and effort. It includes lots of research, patterns, colors, jewelry, hats, shoes, and occasionally even a stage. They all must be period appropriate, from modern day to the Renaissance ages and before.

As for our training, it has been long and extensive for both of us. David has gone from learning the basics from mother and grandmother, to tailoring and clothing details in shops and from seamstresses. Many different people, all with knowledge to share, along with his own twists has shaped David's style into the fine workmanship it is today. He has been sought out by people and companies ranging from doll shop owners to doll manufacturers.

Brian's training led him down a different path. He also has been a very creative individual from a young age. He found his talent come alive through art. Brian does a lot of the building of backdrops, props, and sets. He is intrigued by detail and thrives on being more and more inventive. David may do all of the sewing, but Brian pulls more than his share, with painting, eyelashes, and hair work.

Lucy and Ricky's Anniversary.

D.A.E. Originals
David Escobedo/Brian Schafer
20201 E. Germann
Queen Creek, AZ. 85242
Visit us on the web
http:\\users.aol.com\butricky\dae.htm

Creations by
D.A.E. ORIGINALS

These dolls are a living passion and even an obsession at times. They cause your mind to work, design, and create. In your mind's eye, all you see are beads and lace flying and dancing with fabric, threads, and needles. You can truly get lost. Anyone who enters this insane atmosphere, feels it. When they come to where ever we are, they feel crazy. Now, do people talk about it? No, they accept it.

D.A.E. Originals tries to represent some of the finest doll creations ever offered. Combining classic dress maker techniques with vintage fabrics and design, vintage fur pieces, all natural cottons, silks, linens, woolens, and new age synthetic blends, we create the ultimate pieces for the discriminating buyer and collector. People like shopping for the ultimate in designer dolls and fashion. Creating these dolls is like a means of escape in this hustle and bustle world. It's nice to be painting a small blank face and when she has been totally finished, you step back, and she finally gets to look back at you.

Tinkerbell

Raggedy Ann and Andy

Annette Funicello as a Mouseketeer.

Her First Boyfriend.

DICK TAHSIN

As a famed fashion illustrator, I use my talents to create some of the most highly prized and exclusive customized BARBIE® doll editions offered in the collector's marketplace today. My doll designs are for the collector and admirer who appreciates quality craftsmanship and exclusivity. I design more than just a doll for a client. I create an entire packaged concept.

The eldest of six children born and raised in Cleveland, Ohio, I have been drawing and designing since the age of three. As a Baby Boomer growing up during the Twist 'N Turn era of the BARBIE® doll, I fondly recall clipping the newspaper fashion illustrations and the BARBIE® doll fashion booklet sketches to use as models.

From early on, the BARBIE® doll has been an inspiration in my life. Her wonderful packaging art and color/paper doll book illustrations were clearly a significant factor in shaping my career goal and style.

Forties glamour artists, Alberto Vargas and Fifties fashion

painter Rene Gruau also influenced my artistic style while growing up and winning numerous high school art awards. In 1982 I received a full scholarship to attend the prestigious Fashion Institute of Technology in New York City. There I perfected my craft of fashion illustration and design. Upon graduating, my artistic talent has been utilized by such top fashion designers as Bill Blass, Chanel, Calvin Klein and most notable Ralph Lauren, where I've resided at for the past six years. My extensive BARBIE® doll knowledge, collector criteria, and doll artistry was called upon by Ralph Lauren in the design development and creation of the forthcoming Ralph Lauren BARBIE® doll and Ken® doll exclusive to Bloomingdale's. Working on the Ralph Lauren BARBIE® doll and Ken® doll project was a dream come true for me. It was wonderful to be given cart blanche to develop everything from hair, make-up, and clothing to packaging concepts and copy.

Over the years, many companies besides Polo Ralph Lauren have called upon my artistic vision: 1988 saw my assisting in formulating and launching a popular BARBIE® doll collector's magazine. 1990 brought Mattel requesting my expertise to coordinate the BARBIE® doll's Pink Jubilee 30th Anniversary Gala at Lincoln Center and in 1993 the Delaware Valley Barbie Club elected me to serve as Chairman of the 1996 National Barbie Doll Collector's Convention, BARBIE® and the Bandstand.

I stand alone among my contemporaries due to my all encompassing talents as designer, illustrator, and marketeer of what appears to be some of the most alluring and expensive designer artist dolls on the market today. I love drawing and designing be it a face, costume, or package. I believe my dedication, enthusiasm, and perfectionism reflects in my work and the customer recognizes and respects this.

My dazzling doll artist designs are in fact very special and have been featured by TV's *Entertainment Tonight* and in the

Dick Tahsin
Dick Tahsin Designs
380 Dartmouth Ct.
Bensalem, PA. 19020

pages of *The New York Times* and *USA Today*. They're truly the epitome of design talent at its best. I use only the highest quality materials in my creations and will search to find the perfect scaled print and/or added accessory to compliment the desired look. There's no gaudy ruffles, crocheted stitches, or overly beaded ball gowns here. Stylish, sophisticated, glamourous and glittering, best describe my made-to-order doll designs with the utmost attention paid to details! It's the little things like a hand signed costume label, a miniature working zipper and a perfectly scaled button that I feel brings uniqueness and a sense of couture quality to my designs. I always design thinking what would I like to see being the customer and it's always a BIG picture. It's the entire whole that works and is what people respond to. My design philosophy is great doll, great art, and great

Leading Ladies™, Golden Girl Groups™ and Fifties Flair™ are trademarks of Dick Tahsin Designs.

Bandstand is a trademark of Olive Enterprises, Inc.

box. Clients know that they're purchasing more than just "a doll" from me, they're buying an entire concept...one that's been carefully thought out and executed. Leading Ladies™, Golden Girl Groups™, and Fifties Flair™ are some of the many doll "concept" collections I have produced.

The design process I adhere to is typical of a costume designer for a Broadway show or a Hollywood film of the Golden Era. I submit design sketches to an interested client for approval prior to actually making the finished model. This is done primarily to alleviate any wasted time spent on creating something that will not satisfy the customer. My expressive design sketches show my fashion illustration background and are just as highly prized by some clients as the dolls themselves.

It's my creative concepts, illustration skills, and execution of costume design, makeup, hairstyle, stand, wrist tag, and artful packaging that collectors admire and are willing to pay for when purchasing a dazzling design by designer extraordinaire....Dick Tahsin!

DORINDA BALANECKI

Although my work as a BAR-BIE® doll artesian officially started just two years ago, I've been an active, avid BARBIE® doll creator for nearly 34 years.

I'm a native of Michigan and currently live in the Metropolitan Detroit area. My creative forte has always been in clothing design. My BARBIE® doll creations began when I was five years old, learning to sew on my grandmother's treadle sewing machine. Soon, I was using my mother's sewing machine to create fashions for my own BARBIE® dolls. Later, I studied metal design at Detroit's Center of Creative Studies and I've made my living as a manicurist and nail artist for the past 14 years. All of these skills have given me a great eye for detail and design.

Nine years ago, I became more active in the BARBIE® Doll Collector's Club, Great Lakes Chapter, and also became interested in restoring BARBIE® clothing and accessories. I also began creating "new" fashions using vintage patterns.

My involvement might have stopped there, had I not been given encouragement from my husband, Steve, and three very dear friends, Ivan Burton, Melissa Windham, and MiKelman. These three continue

My husband Steve and I on our wedding day.
I designed and sewed my gown.

to encourage me to experiment with face painting and hair styling.

In 1994, I collaborated with Melissa Windham to create an Erté inspired BARBIE® doll which was auctioned during our annual "BARBIE® Grants A Wish" convention. The doll wore a tight-fitted black evening gown with a train. A black and gold headpiece capped with feathers completed the outfit. The jewelry which adorned the doll was authentic vintage jewelry from the 1920's. For this collaboration, Melissa designed the hair and facial paint while I designed and created the clothing and jewelry.

Since then, Melissa and I have created another Erté design, this time a bridal gown which was auctioned at the 1995 "BARBIE® Grants A Wish" convention. These two dolls brought nearly $900 to the "Grants A Wish" charity, which assists children with chronic illnesses.

On my own, I have created 12 dolls which were used as centerpieces at the 1994 and 1996 BARBIE® National Conventions held in Alabama and Philadelphia, respectively. Photographs of three of my dolls from the 1994 convention have been published in a BARBIE® doll magazine.

In the Spring of 1996, as part of our annual "Grants A Wish" convention, I designed three dolls to represent the State of Alaska in the first-ever all-BARBIE® doll Beauty Pageant created by Ivan Burton. By popular vote, these dolls took first place and a trophy for Best State Costume.

I really enjoy clothing restoration, but I hope to continue to create one-of-a-kind beautiful BARBIE® dolls.

Dorinda Balanecki
3806 Long Meadow Lane
Orion, MI. 48359

I made 32 of this outfit for the 1995 National BARBIE® doll Convention in New Mexico borrowing the design I created for the "1995 BARBIE® Grants A Wish" Souvenir doll.

Photos by Dan Lippit.

Miss Alaska is a total repaint and has a costume designed for the 1996 BARBIE®
"Grants A Wish" beauty pageant. She won!

Photo by Dan Lippit.

Slumber party Teresa was given a new body and total face repaint. Her hair was straightened and the multi-colored raw silk suit was created by me.

Italian BARBIE® doll with a total face repaint.

Photos by Dan Lippit.

Creations by
DORINDA BALANECKI

Fun to Dress Black BARBIE® doll. Total repaint, hairstyle, and dress designed for the 1994 National BARBIE® doll Convention in Alabama. Owned by Scott Romano.

Photo by Dan Lippit.

HOW TO CREATE YOUR OWN FASHION WONDER

Many of the featured artists will agree that learning to create your own beautiful fashion doll creations happens by discovering the trial and error procedure. Experimentation is the most important part of the process, so begin with a lower priced doll before graduating to the more expensive dolls. Once you have purchased a doll the excitement begins.

REMOVING THE HEAD. **(Step 1)** Tools needed: Needle nose pliers.

The first step that you will need to do is remove the head from the doll. This may sound like an easy task, but think again. With the child safety laws, heads are not that easy to just "pop off" on many dolls. Go slowly and you will need a pair of needle nose pliers to gently stretch the vinyl at the back of the neck to get it over the knob, arrow joint, or whatever you may discover. Once the head is removed successfully, the worst is over **(Step 2)**.

(Step 1)

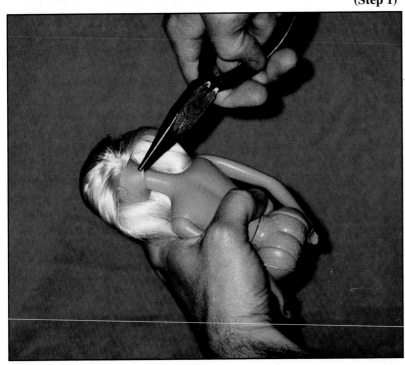

(Step 2)

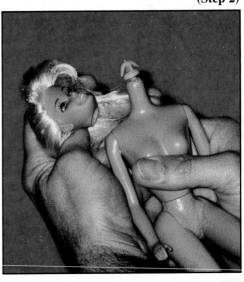

Photos by Kerry Anne Faraone.

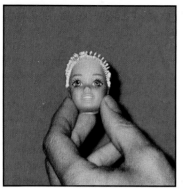

(Step 3)

REROOTING.

Tools needed: Scissors, tweezers, doll hair (which can be bought at craft stores, used from old existing dolls, or be creative and use wool, metallic thread, or whatever may strike your fancy), and a large needle.

(Step 3) To reroot a doll you must first cut all the doll's hair off, cutting it as close to the scalp as possible. Save the hair because you may want to incorporate it in with the new hair, or save it for the reroot of a future doll. **(Step 4)** With a pair of tweezers, go inside the neck opening and pull out all the knotted ends inside the head. It's a tedious job, but all the hair does need to be removed. **(Step 5)** Once the scalp is bare, you can begin the process of rerooting.

(Step 4)

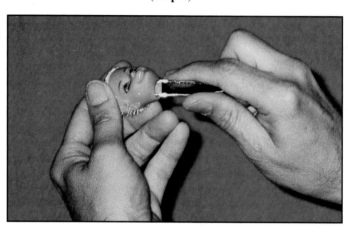

(Step 5)

(Step 6)

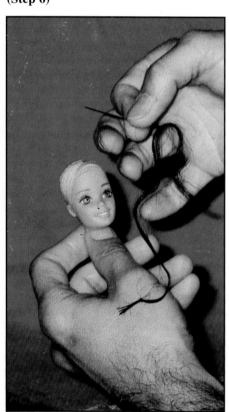

(Step 6) Begin by taking approximately 15-20 strands of hair, thread it through the needle and knot the end. **(Step 7)** Go in through the neck opening and out one of the numerous holes in the scalp. I begin at the crown of the head and work outwardly in a circular pattern until I end at the hairline. Make sure you fill EVERY hole. No cheating, because by skipping holes it will show up in the end product. It's not the most entertainment you'll experience, but hang in there. **(Step 8)** Before you know it, your doll will once again have a full head of hair, whether it be blond, brunette, pink, white, or a mixture of colors.

(Step 7)

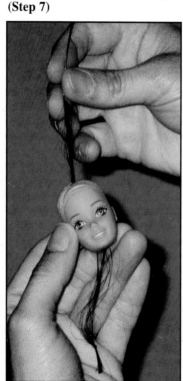

(Step 8)

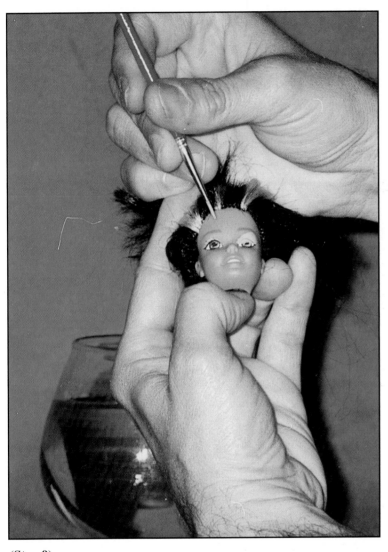

MAKEUP.

Tools needed: Acrylic paint, small paint brushes, a cup of water, paper towel, toothpick, cotton swab, needle, and black thread.

(Step 9) I always begin working on the eyes of the doll first, because this will require the most work and creativity. With a mixture of White and Burnt Sienna, I mix a small batch of paint that comes relatively close to the doll's natural color. Some artists remove all the doll's facial paint, but for the novice designer it's best to use the doll's painted features as some sort of guide line to work with. You will still be repainting over the features, so you're also creating your own look. Plus if you're not careful removing the facial paint, you can remove the doll's skin tone which is one thing you do not want to do.

To begin painting the upper eyelids of the doll (I never like the "just goosed look" on most fashion dolls!) dip your brush into water and roll it into the paint mixture to create a point on your brush. Then paint the desired look you want to create. Don't apply the paint too thickly because you really don't want a just painted look.

(Step 10) In case you make a mistake, you can use your swab or the point of a toothpick to remove any excess paint.

(Step 9)

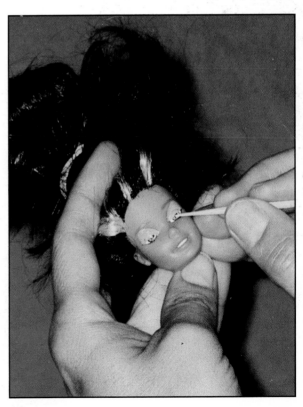

(Step 10)

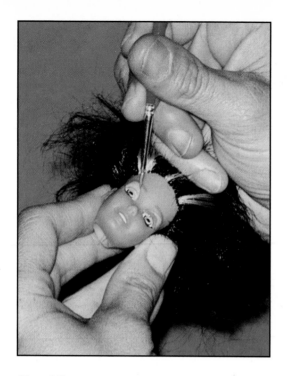

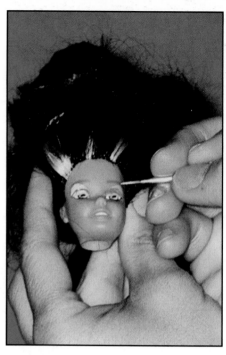

(Step 11)

(Step 12)

(Step 11) After painting the base color, apply a darker shade by adding more Burnt Sienna and carefully paint the crease in the eyelid. This will give your eyes a more natural look.

(Step 12) With a lighter color, (adding more white to the mixture), I begin highlighting the area just above the outside corner of the eye up to the eyebrow. You can also highlight the center area of the eyelid.

(Step 13) Next comes the eye shadow and the color is up to you. Whichever color you decide, don't make it harsh. Colorful eye shadow is great if it's professionally done and blended well. Remember you can tone a color down by adding a little white. Paint the color and once again with white, highlight the center of the eyelid. You can make the makeup as wild or as subdued as you'd like. The excitement is in experimenting.

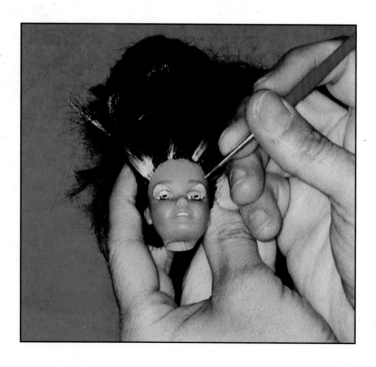

(Step 13)

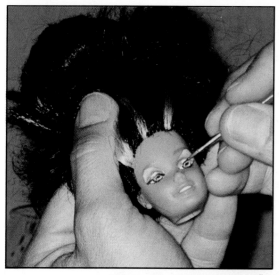

(Step 14)

(Step 14) Once the eyes are painted, with Raw Umber or Black acrylic, paint in the eye liner. Just a thin line above the eye is more than sufficient unless you're creating that television Evangelist.

(Step 15) Painting the lips will be next and this takes extreme patience to get into the corners of the mouth. A magnifying glass will come in handy. With painting the lips, remember to paint the lower lip a hair shade lighter than the upper lip. Not that it's so noticeable, but it will reflect the natural look of lips.

I really don't recommend blush, because if you're not a pro at it, your doll could wind up looking like a circus clown. Leave the doll's natural blush unless you're one to experiment. One friend uses red carbon paper and gently rubs his finger over it, or uses a cotton swab and applies it to the doll's cheeks. It looks great, but too much carbon paper ink could be disastrous.

Once the doll's facial paint is dry (1-2 hours), it's time to apply the eyelashes. **(Step 16)** With your needle and thread, thread the needle and leave it double threaded. Along the eye liner (which has become your guide line) poke the needle into the outer eye corner, **(Step 17)** bring it through the doll's head and out the neck opening. Pull the thread through until the desired length or longer appears above the eye. Knot the thread at the neck opening, cut it and pull the thread back out of the eye lid until the knot is secure behind the eye. Cut the thread a bit longer because you'll trim the eyelashes once they are complete.

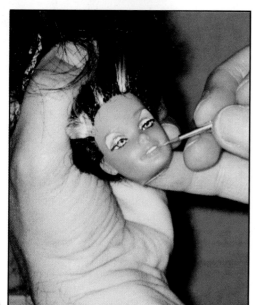

(Step 15)

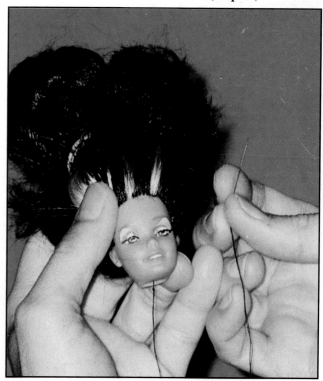

(Step 17)

(Step 16)

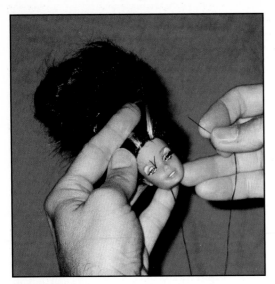

(Step 18)

(Step 19)

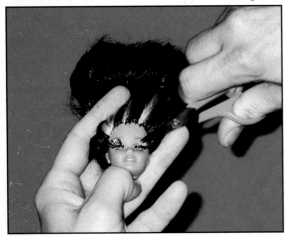

(Step 20)

(Step 18) Repeat this procedure across the eye liner and then move on to the next eye.

(Step 19) Once completed, trim the lashes to give them a natural look. I always trim them extremely short at the inner eye and gradually make them longer toward the outer eye.

(Step 20) You finally completed the look for your doll and it's time to pop the head back on the body which is an easier task than removing the head.

SETTING THE HAIR. Tools needed: Doll brush, small comb, plastic drinking straws, pins and paper towels.

Now it's time to play beautician. The first thing to do is get all your tools ready for this procedure. Take the plastic drinking straws and cut them into miniature rollers. The length of each roller is up to you, although I wouldn't cut them shorter that 3/4 of an inch. Take a paper towel and cut it into small rectangles. These will be used as paper ends, like what you use when you give yourself a home permanent. It will keep the ends of your doll's hair together as you wind it on the roller. You will also need pins to hold the rollers in place. I use the long fashion pins with the "pearl" ends which are easier to grasp when removing the pins. You're now ready to proceed.

(Step 21) I prefer my doll's hair to be styled up, so after brushing the doll's hair to get out any tangles, I make a ponytail at the back or top of the head. I also like bangs, so I leave a few strands loose at the forehead.

(Step 21)

(Step 22)

(Step 23)

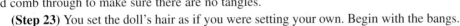

(Step 24)

(**Step 22**) Wet the doll's hair with tap water (keep the temperature of the water average) and comb through to make sure there are no tangles.

(**Step 23**) You set the doll's hair as if you were setting your own. Begin with the bangs. You comb up a strand of hair and cut it to the desired length. I like my doll's to have hair proportioned to their body, so I cut off a good half inch to an inch. When cutting the hair, never cut it straight across, either cut it at an angle or cut it into a pointed arrow. This will avoid that blunt cut, chop job look to your hairstyle. (**Step 24**) Once the strand is cut, wrap the end in the strip of paper towel and (**Step 25**) roll it onto the roller.

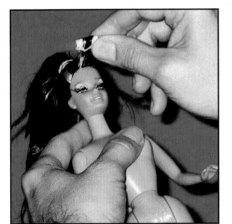
(Step 25)

(**Step 26**) Once rolled, place the pin through the roller and into the doll's head. Avoid sticking the pin into the doll's face as it could leave a pin prick in the vinyl. Make sure the pin goes into the scalp.

(**Step 27**) Before continuing you'll want to hide the rubber band that is used for the ponytail. Take a strand of hair and wrap it around the rubber band and tuck the end into the rubber band.

(Step 26)

(**Steps 28 & 29**) Continue setting the hair until all the hair is wrapped, rolled, and pinned into place. (If you prefer to have your hair in a flowing down style, set the hair as you would your own. If you would like it sweeping over to the right, then set the hair with the rollers going to the right. If you like straight bangs, just tape them down. There's no limit to what you can create. It just takes practice and experimentation.

(Step 29)

(Step 27)

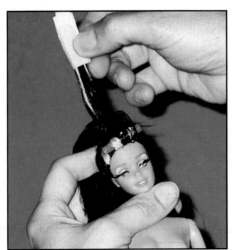
(Step 28)

(Step 30)

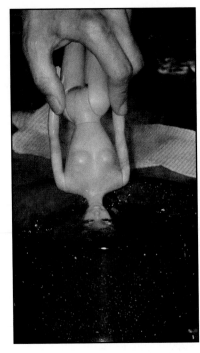

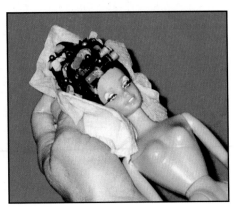

(Step 32)

(Step 30) Now that your doll's hair is set, it's time to trim any fly away hairs that are sticking out. Even though you did a perfect job at setting the hair, there's always a few pieces that refuse to play by the rules.

(Step 31) It's now time for your doll's torture treatment. Take a saucepan of water and heat it until it thoroughly bubbles. Place the doll's head into the boiling water for just 15 seconds, any longer will give you a frizz job that you wouldn't believe. I know that from experience, so I'll save you that trial and error experience.

(Step 32) Take the doll's head out of the water, blot it dry with a paper towel and let it dry overnight.

(Step 33)

REDOING THE BODY. Tools needed: an Exacto knife.

While your doll's hair is drying, don't think there's time to relax. Turn off the television and get back to work.

(Step 33) There's not a lot you can do with the body, but you can work wonders on the arms, hands, and fingers of your creations. With an Exacto knife slice a few fingers of your doll. Go easy through the crease of the doll's indented finger separations. Don't cut each and every finger unless you haven't had a cup of coffee in twenty years and are as steady as a rock. This is suppose to be fun, not a project to cause stress.

(Step 34) Once you have completed this operation it's back to the boiling water for your doll. Start by placing the upper arm into the boiling water for 3 seconds. (Step 35) Remove the arm and bend it to the desired angle and (Step 36) then immediately (still holding the doll's arm in position) run it under cold tap water. Voila, the arm will stay in that position, or Voila, you just messed up. Don't panic, just repeat the procedure and bend again.

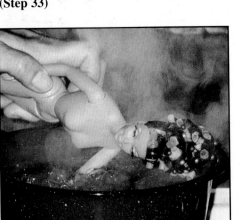

(Step 34)

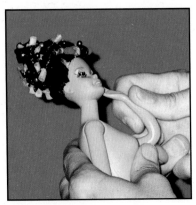

(Step 35)

(Step 36)

(Step 37)

(Step 38)

(Step 39)

(Step 40)

(Step 41)

(Step 42)

(Step 43)

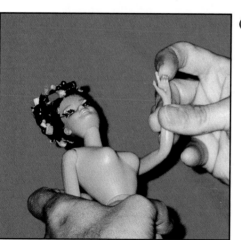

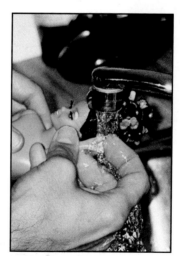

(Step 37) Next move on to the wrist. Submerge just the wrist into the boiling water, wait 3 seconds, **(Step 38)** bend the wrist and **(Step 39)** hit the cold water.

(Step 40) You should have this procedure down by now, so let's do the fingers. Dip the fingers into the boiling water for 3 seconds, **(Step 41)** bend them and **(Step 42)** run them under cold water.

(Step 43) Don't go crazy with your new bending experience and bend your doll into a pretzel. Try to give your doll a natural look even though there's many unnatural looking gestures out there.

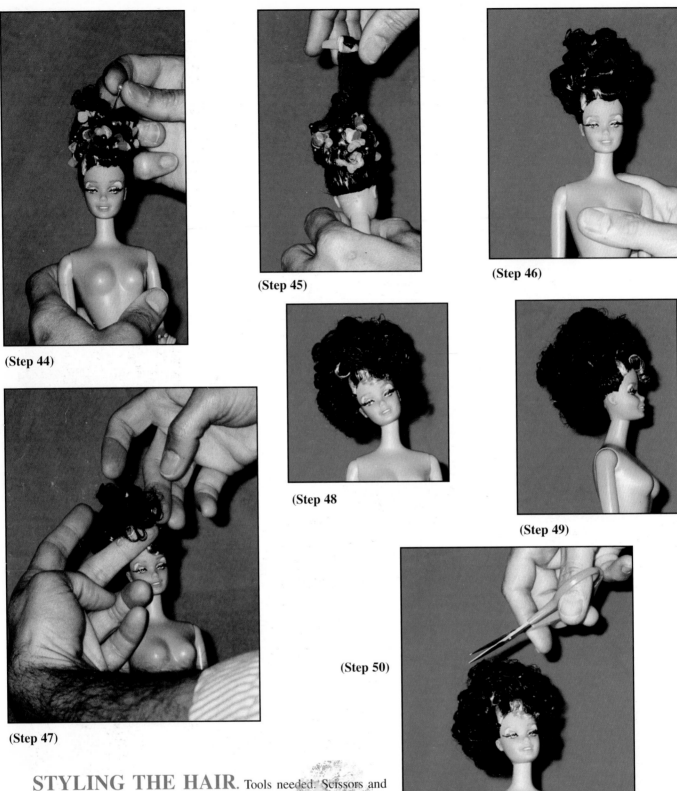

(Step 44)

(Step 45)

(Step 46)

(Step 48

(Step 49)

(Step 47)

(Step 50)

STYLING THE HAIR. Tools needed. Scissors and comb.

(Step 44) Once the doll's hair is dry, remove the pin from the roller and gently unwind the hair. (Step 45) Then proceed to the next roller.

(Step 46) Once all the rollers are removed, you can leave the hair in its Grecian curl look or to create a much softer look you can (Step 47) fan out each curl with your fingertips. You could use a comb or brush, but I wouldn't recommend continuously combing or brushing the curl out as it could tend to frizz the hair. A gentle brushing once or twice will do, but don't over do it.

(Steps 48 & 49) You now have a new look to your doll's hair. (Step 50) Trim away any flyaway hairs. You will be able to recut the hair once your outfit is complete.

PREPARING TO CREATE AN OUTFIT. Tools need-
ed: Two 2 inch brass eye pins, stretch mesh fabric, needle nose plyers, needle, and thread.

(Step 51) The first thing to do is to place the 2 inch brass eye pin into the doll's old earring hole and out the hole of the other ear. (Step 52) (If your doll has no ear holes, in the accessories section it will give you other ideas on creating earrings) (Step 53) With your needle nose plyers, clip the end of the eye pin and loop the end matching the other side. (Step 54) Now you have your set loops for hanging your designed earrings which you'll learn in the accessories section.

(Step 55) If your outfit is going to be a tight fitting ensemble, you may want to do the stockings next. I found that stretch, sheer material or fine stretch mesh make won-derful stockings. Cut a strip about 1 inch wide and enough length to go mid thigh and wrap the material around the doll's leg closing it at the back of the thigh. Using needle and thread, begin at the top and overhand stitch a seam down the leg.

(Step 56) When you get down to the doll's ankle, trim the two side flaps and continue sewing, ending at the bottom of the doll's foot. (Step 57) You now have a great pair of stockings to enhance your doll's outfit. (Step 58)

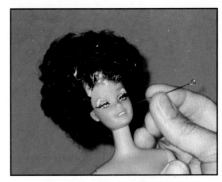

(Step 51)

(Step 52)

(Step 53)

(Step 54)

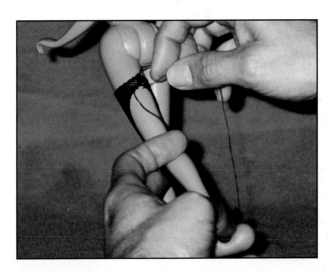

(Step 55)

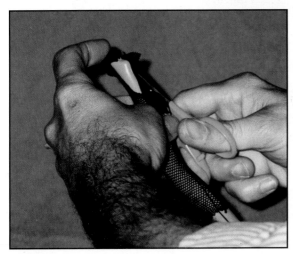

(Step 56)

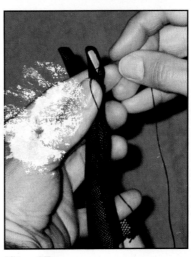

(Step 57)

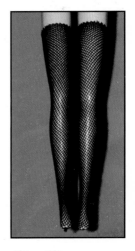

(Step 58)

DESIGNING AN OUTFIT. Tools needed: Your imagination.

I'm not going to tell you how to design an outfit because that will only stifle your creative juices. The outfit you design is your idea and your idea alone. I will give you some tips though to help you with your designing adventure.

You'll need to start off with a pattern, unless you're one of those talented individuals who can create your own patterns. Patterns for fashion dolls can be found in any fabric or craft shop, or any store with a craft section. Though the patterns of today don't exactly have the perfect fit, they may require you to make a few adjustments to achieve the look that you like.

Look for older fashion doll patterns at doll shows and thrift shops. Finding one complete is not easy, but not an impossibility. You'll discover that the older patterns have a much better fit on the dolls.

Once you find some patterns, become a "pattern masher". That's when you take the top of one pattern, the bottom of another pattern and the sleeves of yet another pattern and piece them together. Make your outfit special and not a carbon copy of the original pattern.

You're now ready and anxious to run to the fabric store and select 5,000 yards of different material to work with. Wrong! You can create an outfit with just 1/2 yard of material and why does everyone think, fabric....a fabric store! Go for the unusual and go to thrift shops and look through the vintage clothes for material that you'd like. In most thrift shops the clothes are very inexpensive and there's more than a 1/2 a yard even in a skirt. This way you won't have the same exact fabric that 200 other designers have. Not that you'll have a solo find, but it's less likely that everyone else will find that same fabric.

Be careful when choosing fabric texture and print. Keep in mind that the texture and print should be in proportion to the doll. A thick wool made into a coat will look like your doll got lost in a rolled up rug. (Although I've seen many talented individuals create wonderful outfits with over-sized textures and prints. They have the knowledge and experience to make it work.) There's a wide variety of fabric with small print so don't feel that it's an impossibility to find any. I guarantee you won't have a problem with that.

Read your patterns thoroughly and understand each step before you begin to sew. Even I have a problem with the "I know how to do this part" syndrome only to discover that I place the sleeves on backwards and it's not exactly paradise ripping out those small stitches.

Enjoy what you're doing and create with your imagination.

ACCESSORIZING YOUR DOLL. Tools needed: 2 inch brass head pins, needle and thread, craft wire, beads, trinkets, jewelry clasps or hook, jump ring, needle nose pliers, shoes, and once again, your imagination.

Before you start accessorizing your doll, you may want to give your doll's hair a final cutting to suit the outfit. **(Step 59)** You can cut the hair without losing the curl by clipping it above the last curl at the bottom of the strand of hair. Cut below that curl and you're going to have a piece of straight hair sticking straight out.

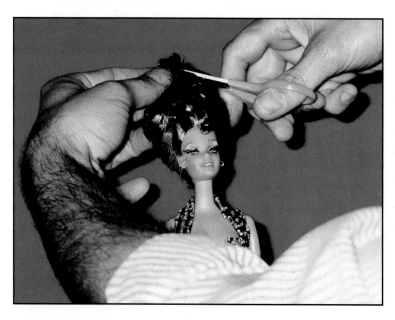

(Step 59)

(Step 60)

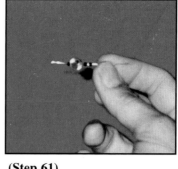

(Step 61)

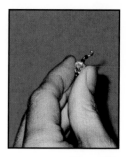

(Step 62)

(**Step 60**) Once the doll's hair is to your liking and you have protected the doll's face with a paper towel, lightly spray it with hairspray. This is not a necessity, but with traveling around to do shows, and the packing and unpacking of dolls, it's just a precaution. Don't overspray it unless you want to create a '60s beehive plastered look.

Jewelry is always a fun part to do. It let's you know that your creation is nearly done. Since the doll already has her set loops for the earrings, we'll start with those. (**Step 61**) Take the 2 inch brass head pin and thread on beads, crystals, or whatever you desire in your design. (**Step 62**) Snip the end with your needle nose plyers and make a loop at the end. This loop will be connected with the loop already on the doll (**Step 63**) creating a wonderful pair of earrings. If your doll has no ear holes, you can take the long pin with the "pearl" end (used for rolling the hair), snip off about a 1/2 inch from the point and insert the pin into the ear lobe. If you prefer dangling earrings, simply hang a dangling charm, or design your own trinket with the 2 inch head pin and place it onto the pin before inserting it into the doll's ear lobe.

For dolls that have rather large ear holes in their ears where the old earrings existed, some designers place a round toothpick into the hole, cut it to the ear lobe and then insert the pin into the wood. If you're not artistic, glue a sequin or bead to the ear.

Creating a bracelet is your next step. (**Step 64**) Simply take a strip of crafting wire and cut off a 4 inch piece. (**Step 65**) Thread a sead bead onto the wire and wrap the wire around it to set it in place. (**Step 66**) Thread on more beads

(Step 63)

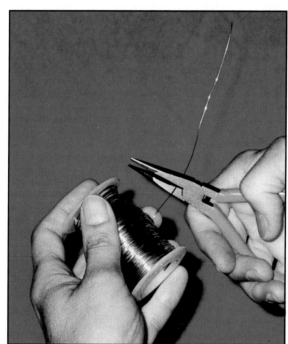

(Step 64)

(Step 65)

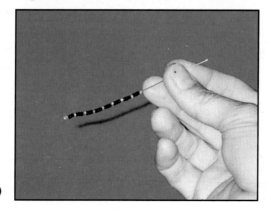

(Step 66)

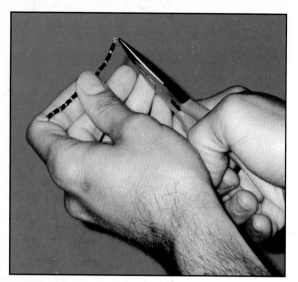

(Step 67)

creating your own design and **(Step 67)** wrap the remaining wire around the last bead, clipping off the excess wire.

(Step 68) Wrap the beaded wire around the doll's wrist and you have an instant bracelet. You can use this same technique to create a choker for the doll's neck.

Necklaces can be a bit trickier to create. Finding a tiny necklace hook or clasp isn't easily. You may have to check with a jeweler for these.

(Step 69) Double thread a needle by threading the two loose ends into the eye of the needle. This will create a large loop at the end of the thread instead of a knot. Take the needle and thread and go through the eye of the jewelry hook. Bring your needle through the loop of the thread and secure the jewelry hook in place. **(Step 70)** Have fun threading beads and crystals creating your own unique look. **(Step 71)** When you reach the desired length, knot a tiny jump ring onto the end and **(Step 72)** run your needle and thread back through the beads and clip the excess thread. This procedure will hide the usual knot and raw edges seen at the ends of necklaces. **(Step 73)** You have just created another accessory for your doll.

(Step 74) Another final touch is the doll's fingernails. With acrylic paint, dab on the nail color which should match the color of the lipstick you previously painted.

The barefoot Contessa now needs shoes and don't attempt to try and make your own. There are plenty of mass marketed shoes to choose from. You can certainly embellish the shoes to give them your own distinct look. Coat the tip of the shoe with craft glue. **(Step 75)**

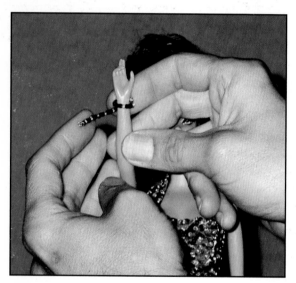

(Step 68)

(Step 69)

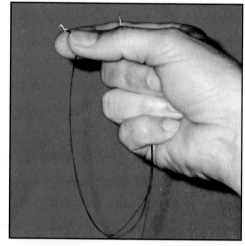

(Step 70)

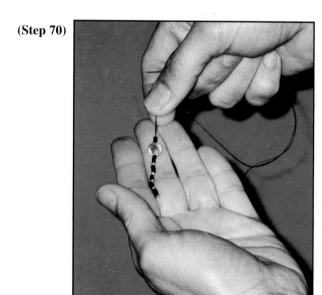

(Step 71)

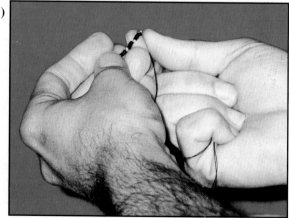

(Step 72)

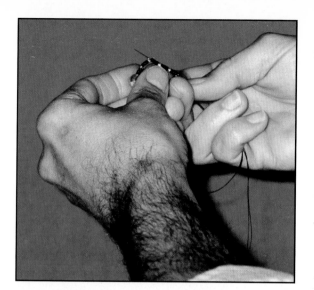

(Step 73)

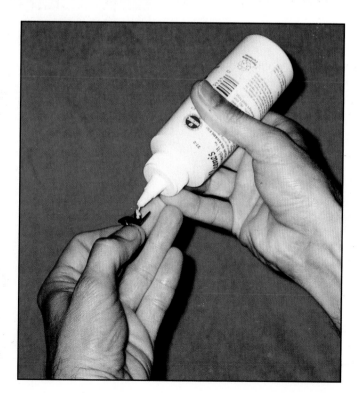

(Step 74)

(Step 75)

Sprinkle on some glitter, pat it down, and sprinkle again. (Step 76) Let the shoes dry overnight and then coat them with clear nail polish. This will keep the glitter from chipping off in little pieces. You don't have to do all your shoes with glitter. There's pearlized craft paint, glue on tiny flowers or pom-poms. Try your hand at gluing fabric onto the shoes. Once again the ideas are endless.

(Step 77) Other finishing touches to complete the look are gloves, fur stoles, feather boas, handbags, fans, books, or whatever you feel would enhance your creation. Many miniature items can be found in craft stores, although it's fun to try to create your own. Just don't over do it with the accessories. Sometimes less is more.

(Step 76)

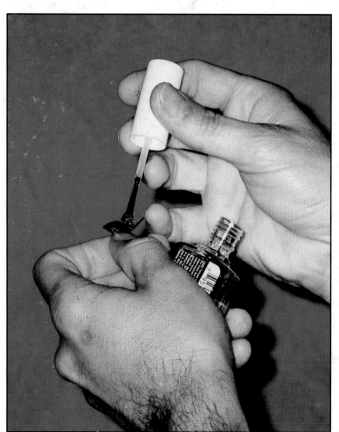

(Step 77)

(Step 78)

(Steps 79 & 80) Now you can look back at the doll you bought and see the transformation you created. You turned a mass marketed doll into a one-of-a-kind marvel. Be proud of yourself and prepare yourself for your next creation.

(Step 80)

(Step 79)

MARKETING YOUR CREATIONS.

Once you start creating you'll get hooked and everyone in your family will receive tons of dolls. Whether they collect or not, you'll give your fashion creations as gifts for Christmas, Birthdays, Anniversaries, Bar Mitzvahs, Christenings, Weddings, etc. You'll want everyone to have one of your masterpieces even though a few friends and family members will happily display them at their next garage sale. Don't let the non-excitement of others get you down. There are a number of collectors who would be very interested in your work if it's professionally created and presented.

Though you created the look of the doll, the doll is not actually your doll. A manufacturer did create the doll and has a trademark and copyright on it. You should never use the doll's trademark name in any advertising you do. You create the outfits for fashion dolls and enhance their looks. You should have the recognition for all your hard redesigning work. Some artists make wrist tags to place on the doll. Others have tags on their outfits which state the garment is their original design. Some actually sign the doll in permanent ink, while some sign the doll stands. This is your second market redux creation and you deserve the acknowledgment.

(Step 81) Most artists/designers have come up with their own designer boxes. Many just purchase boxes from gift shops and design their own logo on the front. You can also look up a box wholesale company to order boxes, but since you're just starting out, stick with the boxes at gift shops. Unless several of you get together, order the boxes and divide them up amongst yourselves. If you're going to do a lot of shows and travel around, it may be wise to check into collapsible boxes which are much easier to store and cart around.

You're now ready to hit the retail circuit. The important thing is to market your creations. Try advertising in a doll magazine, attending doll shows, printing flyers, or word of mouth. No matter how you decide to get the word out, the main ingredient is to get yourself and your work known. Don't expect anyone to come knocking at your door, making you an instant "celebrity", that only happens in the movies. Have business cards made up. Self promotion is very important, yet don't come across as a swell headed egotist. That can destroy one's dreams in a flash. Be yourself and you'll never go wrong.

Before you start hearing from all your "fans", you should start thinking about pricing your work. This is as bad as discussing politics or religion. No one can tell you what price you should sell your creations for. That will have to be determined by you and it's a "Catch 22". You don't want to overprice yourself out of the market, but you don't want to sell yourself short. Take into consideration the work and time it takes to create a finished piece. Most of the artists in this book require two full days to finish one doll, if not longer. There's a lot of work that goes into one doll and sometimes the collector doesn't realize that. That's why communication with the collectors is important and they truly enjoy hearing how you created the doll's look and ensemble. I have met so many new friends by talking with collectors at my booth. Notice I never answered the question about pricing? I will say that the range in prices of the artist's creations featured in this book is $35 - $2,000 depending on the work involved with each doll and outfit. It does not mean that the $35 doll is not as nice as the $2,000 doll because that doesn't hold true. Beauty is in the eye of the beholder and I have seen creations of all price ranges that I would love to have in my collection.

Create what you enjoy and you will never go wrong. You can never guess the second market. You may find that at one show the collectors are interested in one certain look and at another show they're after something else. Don't get the impression that since you made a lot of pretty doll creations that everyone will just have to buy one. There's a lot of competition out there. It's a gamble, just like the big manufacturers gamble with a new product.

It may sound like I'm discouraging you, but in reality I'm not by any means. I'm just trying to relay the message of what you could experience if you decide to market your creations. I have seen too many talented individuals become discouraged, burnt out, and dismayed because their dreams were bigger than reality. Unfortunately they no longer create and the loss of their beautiful craftsmanship is truly a shame. By all means have those dreams because dreams keep us going, but keep those dreams in prospective. It took many of the artists/designers in this book years before they achieved the true recognition they deserved. Create for yourself first and for the love of designing. If you believe in something, then go for the gold and learn from all your mistakes along the way. Things don't happen overnight, but they do happen.

Hopefully I've inspired many of you to try your hand at creating. Even if it's for self enjoyment or refurbishing one of your childhood treasures. The world of fashion can be an inspirational experience and the sky is the limit. Keep creating!

(Step 81)